Nabi ﷺ's love for children

his teaching and nurturing them

By
**Moulana Abu Talha Muhammed
Izharul Hasan Mahmood**

Translation edited by:
Mufti A.H Elias
(May Allah Protect him)

Fourth Authorized Edition 2012

Title	:	Nabi ﷺ's Love for Children
By	:	Moulana Abu Talha Muhammad Izharul Hasan Mahmood
Translation edited by	:	Mufti A.H Elias
Second Published	:	November 2012
Pages	:	104

Published By:

Zam Zam Publishers

Urdu Bazar Karachi-Pakistan.
Ph : 0092-21-32760374
0092-21-32761671
Fax : 0092-21-32761673
E-mail : zamzam01@cyber.net.pk

Visit Our Website

Www.zamzam Publishers.com

Books Also Available in :

❈ united Kingdom

AL-FAROOQ-INTERNATIONAL
Leicester

AZHAR ACADEMY LTD.
London E12 5QA

ISLAMIC BOOK CENTER
Bolton Bll 3NE

❈ U.S.A

ZEENAT EMPORIUM
Chicago

❈ south Africa

AL-HUDA PUBLICATIONS
Johannesburg

Table of Contents

PREFACE

All praise is due only to Allaah. We laud Him and beseech His aid and beg forgiveness only from Him and believe in Him and rely solely on Him. We seek salvation in Him from the evils of our inner selves and the vices of our actions. There is none to misguide one whom Allaah intends to guide. I bear witness that there is no one worthy of worship but Allaah, the One who has no partner. I also testify that Hadhrat Muhammad ﷺ is the faithful servant and the Last Rasul of Allaah. May Allaah Ta'ala's mercy be on him, his family and his Sahabaah ﵁ and may He bless them and raise their status.

Hadhrat Moulana Izhaarul Hasan Mahmood has adequately substantiated from the Sunnat and Ahadith the par- excellent beautiful teachings of Rasulullaah ﷺ concerning the love, upbringing and nurturing of children. The rights of children, namely:-

1.) Showing kindness and affection to them;
2.) Displaying joy on birth of daughters;
3.) Praying and seeking forgiveness for them;
4.) Granting them gifts;
5.) Sharing their moments of joy, grief and happiness;
6.) Calling the Adhaan on birth and doing the 'takhneek' for them;
7.) Playing, kissing, hugging, lifting them up, joking, respecting, aiding, interceding, mounting them on his mount, smiling, taking permission from them, shedding tears when they die, protecting their lives

irrespective whether Muslim or non- Muslim, crying with them, greeting them, carrying new born babies on his lap, make them race and rewarding them, be informal with them, console them, advising them and teaching them with love and affection.

The able author has mentioned the interaction between beloved Nabi ﷺ and his own children and grand children.

Also many interesting authentic stories including:-

1.) A lengthy narration explaining in detail how Hadhrat Salmaan Farsi ﷺ accepted Islaam and

2.) The incident of the youth of Tauheed as stated in Surah Burooj.

Then recording the events surrounding the 5 who spoke miraculously as babies namely:-

1.) The fortunate child from Yamaamah during Hajj;

2.) The child of the mother whom Pharouh executed unjustly;

3.) Hadhrat Essa ﷺ on birth;

4.) The child who spoke to free Juraji from sin;

5.) A child from the Bani Israeel.

One should not forget that Nabi ﷺ spoke praising Allaah Ta'ala on birth. Then concluding the book by:-

1.) A section on virtues of Durood;

2.) A section on stories relating to the parents rights over children and

3.) A section on the saying pertaining to parents rights over children.

Many books have been written on children upbringing but this explains interaction with na-baligh (immature) children.

May Allaah Jalla Majdahu accept the effort of the respected author and all those who aided in this most valuable work.

A.H.Elias (Mufti)
Muharram 1431
January 2010

FOREWORD

One evening whilst partaking meals with my children, I narrated to them the incident of that fortunate young Sahabi ﵁ who was partaking meals with Rasulullaah ﷺ. During the course of the meal this Sahabi began eating from all sides of the utensil, so Nabi ﷺ taught him three etiquettes of eating, he told him, "Begin eating by taking the name of Allaah. Eat using the right hand and eat from that which is in front of you." (Bukhari)

My son Talha and his younger sister sat and listened attentively and they also made apparent their desire to hear more such incidents. The thought immediately struck me that I should gather such incidents and sayings from the life of Nabi ﷺ which teach us how to interact with children and give them the correct upbringing so that this could reach every child and their pure hearts could be filled with the greatness of Rasulullaah ﷺ and they could bring his Sunnats into their lives.

Our beloved Nabi ﷺ has taught us that children, whether boys or girls, are a bounty from Allaah and should therefore not be treated in a manner where preference is given to one over the other. They should be nurtured in such a way that they firmly believe obedience of Allaah and his Rasul ﷺ to be the absolute truth. Similarly they should make good deeds their hallmark and understand their honour dignity to be only in Deen. May Allaah give all of us the ability to practice. Aameen.

Abu Talha Muhammed Izhaarul-Hasan Mahmood
Markazi Jami Masjid Block, Johar Abaad

Nabi ﷺ's Love *for* children and his teaching and nurturing them

Nabi' ﷺ's love towards his children:

Remember well, our beloved Nabi ﷺ was an embodiment of kindness towards all mankind, but his affection for his own children knew no bounds.

Khadijah رضى الله تعالى عنها bore him four daughters and two sons, whilst Maariyah Qibtiyah رضى الله تعالى عنها bore him one son who was named Ibrahim after his forefather Ibrahim عليه الصلاة والسلام. (This was the total number of his children. All three sons passed away during their infancy.)

Love for Hadhrat Qasim and Hadhrat Abdullah رضى الله تعالى عنه

Nabi ﷺ was very fond of his son Qasim and it was for this very reason that he had given himself the title, Abul-Qasim. When this flower from the garden of Nubuwwat reached the age of walking, he passed away.

On one occasion Nabi ﷺ saw his beloved wife Khadijah رضى الله تعالى عنها very grieved. Upon enquir she said, "How nice would it have been, if our son Qasim had only completed the duration of breastfeeding?" Nabiﷺ consoled her saying, "O Khadijah, Allaah has appointed a wet nurse in Jannat to complete his period of breastfeeding!"

Abdullah was born after him and he had the titles, Tayyib and Taahir. This son also passed away at a very tender age.

The birth and death of Ibrahim رضى الله تعالى عنه

When Abu Raf'i رضى الله تعالى عنه, the slave of Nabi ﷺ brought the good news of the birth of a son, Nabi ﷺ immediately set him free on hearing this good news. (Madaarijun-Nubuwwah *vol.2 pg.773*) This son enjoyed a very short worldly life.

A short while before his demise, Nabi ﷺ had gone to visit him and had taken him in his blessed lap and held him to his bosom. He breathed his last in the very lap of Rasulullaah ﷺ.

The eyes of our beloved Nabi ﷺ swelled with tears which flowed. A Sahabi رضى الله تعالى عنه standing nearby said, "Are you crying O Rasul- Messenger of Allaah ﷺ?"

In a narration of Shamaail-e-Thirmizi it is mentioned that Hadhrat Umme Aiman رضى الله تعالى عنها began to cry out aloud. Nabi ﷺ said, "Why are you crying in this manner in the presence of the Rasul of Allaah? She said, "But you are also crying, O Rasulullaah ﷺ."Nabi ﷺ answered her thus, "Crying is as a result of mercy in the heart. (In other words we should not wail.) O Ibrahim, we are undoubtedly grieved by your demise. Our eyes shed tears and our heart is grief stricken, but our tongues will only utter that which pleases our Rabb." *(Bukhari)*

Hadhrat Anas رضي الله تعالى عنه says that he had never seen anyone show more kindness to their family than Nabi ﷺ. (Madaarijun-Nubuwwah *vol.2 pg.774*)

The face of Nabi ﷺ brimmed with happiness on the occasion of the birth of his daughter:

Hadhrat Umme Aiman رضي الله تعالى عنها was rushing through the market place when she met Hadhrat Sulaimah Khuza'iyah رضي الله تعالى عنها who asked her;

"O Umme Aiman رضي الله تعالى عنها, what makes you so happy? And why are you in such a hurry?"

Hadhrat Umme Aiman رضي الله تعالى عنها said;
"I am off to the most truthful person to give him the good news of the birth of his fourth daughter from Hadhrat Khadijah رضي الله تعالى عنها."

Sulaimah رضي الله تعالى عنها was astonished. Fourth daughter...good news? What is all this? Umme Aiman رضي الله تعالى عنها then explained saying, "This question of yours reminds me of the day when Hadhrat Khadijah رضي الله تعالى عنها gave birth to the first daughter of Nabi ﷺ, Zainab رضي الله تعالى عنها, and **I was asked to inform him of her birth.** I went to him fearing the worst. Fearing I might be buried alive with her. Upon arriving there a most strange thing happened." Sulaimah رضي الله تعالى عنها asked, "And what was that?" Umme Aiman رضي الله تعالى عنها said, **"When I informed Nabi ﷺ of the birth of a daughter, his face brimmed with happiness! Nabi ﷺ came and picked up the child placing** her in his lap. He then kissed her and congratulated her **mother.** Nabi ﷺ thereafter sacrificed an animal and celebrated her birth. Undoubtedly this was something absolutely strange and new amongst the Arabs. A new born was given an increased life span and a new and radiant revolution had taken place!" (Inculcate the love of Nabi ﷺ in the heart of your children. *Pg.26*)

His ﷺ love for his eldest daughter Zainab رَضِىَ اللهُ تَعَالَى عَنْهَا:

Beloved children,

The seal of Nabuwaat-Prophethood ﷺ was blessed with four daughter the eldest being Zainabرَضِىَ اللهُ تَعَالَى عَنْهَا. Nabiﷺ nurtured her in a most unique manner. Her mother Hadhrat Khadijah رَضِىَ اللهُ تَعَالَى عَنْهَا brought her up with honour and in pure environment.

She was later married off to her mother's sister's son, Abul-Aas Ibn Rabee. He was not yet a Muslim when the battle of Badr took place where he was also taken in amongst the captives and brought before Nabi ﷺ. When his family members began to gather the ransom required for his freedom, his faithful wife, the beloved daughter of Rasulullaah ﷺ, Zainab رَضِىَ اللهُ تَعَالَى عَنْهَا presented a valuable necklace of hers as part of the ransom. When this ransom was brought to Nabi ﷺ, taking the necklace into his hand, he began crying as this was in reality originally the necklace of Hadhrat Khadijah رَضِىَ اللهُ تَعَالَى عَنْهَا, which was given to her daughter as a gift at the time of her marriage. **Seeing this necklace, reminded Nabi ﷺ of his faithful wife Khadijah رَضِىَ اللهُ تَعَالَى عَنْهَا, and brought tears to his eyes. He then asked the Sahaba رَضِىَ اللهُ تَعَالَى عَنْهُم if he could free him without any ransom. They unanimously willingly** agreed. **It was not long after that he (Abul-Aas) accepted Islaam and migrated to Madeenah from Makkah.**

Upon the demise of Zainab رضى الله تعالى عنها Nabi ﷺ was very much grieved and due to deeply embedded love, tears flowed from his eyes and he said,

"Zainab رضى الله تعالى عنها was the best of my daughters, who was persecuted because of her love for me."

He even gave his personal shawl as part of the kafn to be used for her, so that perhaps she may be enshrouded by the mercy of Allaah. (Madaarijun-Nubuwwah)

His love for Hadhrat Ruqayyah رضى الله تعالى عنها:

Just as he was affectionate towards his eldest daughter, Nabi ﷺ was affectionate towards his middle daughter, Hadhrat Ruqayyah رضى الله تعالى عنها. She was honoured to marry a noble Sahabi, Hadhrat Uthmaan رضى الله تعالى عنه. On the occasion of the battle of Badr her health had deteriorated, therefore Nabi ﷺ ordered Hadhrat Uthmaan رضى الله تعالى عنه to remain behind and take care of her. Her condition did not improve though, and at a days journey away, on the victorious return of Nabi ﷺ from the battle of Badr, she passed away and was buried.

When Nabi ﷺ later returned and asked regarding her well being, he was informed of her demise which brought tears to his eyes. **He then went to her graveside and stood there for a long time crying and supplicating for her forgiveness and for her stages to be elevated in the hereafter. (Al-Isabah)**

After her demise Uthmaan رضى الله تعالى عنه asked Nabi ﷺ, "What calamity has befallen me, that I have been separated from your beloved daughter who was united in marriage to me, and I am now deprived of this honour?" Nabi ﷺ consoled him and comforted him by giving him his other daughter, Hadhrat Umme Kulthoom رضي الله تعالى عنها. This is why he was known as Zun-Nurain.

His love for Umme Kulthoom رضي الله تعالى عنها:

Nabi ﷺ was very fond of her and he regularly sent her gifts and food items. When she also passed away, the most kind and noble father ever to set foot on earth, **Nabi ﷺ, gave her his own cloth as kafn and he lead her janazah salah.** When Hadhrat Abu Talha رضي الله تعالى عنه was lowering her into her grave, he noticed the eyes of Nabiﷺ full of tears and he saw his lips moving with words of supplication. *(Shamaail-e-Thirmizi)*

His love for Hadhrat Fatima رضي الله تعالى عنها:

As you are all well aware, the fourth and the youngest amongst the daughters of Nabi ﷺ, was Hadhrat Fatima رضي الله تعالى عنها. Just as parents generally are most fond of the youngest children, similarly Nabi's ﷺ love for her knew no bounds.

Whenever he embarked on or returned from a journey, he would visit her. He once told her, **"Fatima, you are a piece of my liver! Whosoever upsets you has upset me!"** on another occasion he said, "Fatima is indeed most beloved to me." *(Mishkat)*

It has been narrated that whenever Hadhrat Fatima رضي الله تعالى عنها visited, Nabi ﷺ would stand up, kiss her hand, ask regarding her well being and make her sit on his place!

Similarly, whenever Nabi ﷺ visited her, she would stand up, welcome her beloved father, kiss his blessed hands and make him sit on her place! *(Abu-Dawud)*

Affection for his ﷺ grandchildren:

Read on about the unmatched love displayed by Nabi ﷺ towards his grandchildren and the manner in which he gave them due regard.

Love shown towards Umaamah رضى الله تعالى عنها:

Hadhrat Umaamah رضى الله تعالى عنها was the daughter of the eldest daughter of Nabi ﷺ, Zainab رضى الله تعالى عنها. She was a splitting image of her mother and Nabi ﷺ had great love for her. She remained in his care for a long time after the demise of her mother. **Nabi ﷺ would play with her and carry her on his lap. When the time of salah would set in, he would place her on his blessed shoulders and perform salah.** When going into ruku he would gently place her on the ground. *(Bukhari and Muslim)*

On one occasion the king of Abyssinia sent a ring as a gift to Nabi ﷺ. Nabi ﷺ announced that he would give the ring to such a person who is most beloved to him. Every person eagerly anticipated being that honoured being, but Nabi ﷺ granted this honour to his beloved grand-daughter Hadhrat Umaamah رضى الله تعالى عنها. *(Al-Isabah)*

Beloved children, hav you not read how much love Nabi ﷺ showed towards children? And, how much he considered them? Now you can well imagine how much love the children had for him.

What a beautiful ride:

Once Nabi ﷺ placed Hadhrat Hasan رضي الله تعالى عنه on his blessed shoulders and walked through the alleys of Madeenah. Seeing this spectacle, a Sahabi رضي الله تعالى عنه commented, "What a beautiful ride!" Nabi ﷺ hearing this said, "And indeed what a beautiful rider!" *(Bukhari)*

It has been reported on the authority of the book Abu-Dawud that Abu Raf'i رضي الله تعالى عنه narrates from his father that he had seen Nabi ﷺ personally call out the azaan in the ears of Hadhrat Husain ﷺ at the time of his birth to Hadhrat Fatima رضي الله تعالى عنها. *(Abu-Dawud)*

I do not like to be separated from Hadhrat Husain رضي الله تعالى عنه:

Nabi ﷺ was once performing salah. When he went into the position of sajdah, Hadhrat Husain رضي الله تعالى عنه jumped on to his back. Nabi ﷺ remained in sajdah for a long time until Hadhrat Husain رضي الله تعالى عنه jumped off. Upon completion of the salah someone inquired as to why the sajdah was so long. Nabi ﷺ then said, "Whilst in sajdah my beloved, Husain رضي الله عنه, climbed onto my back and I did not like the idea of being separated from him, I therefore remained in sajdah for a long time!" *(Bukhari and Muslim)*

Nabi ﷺ once made the following dua for Hadhrat Hasan رضي الله تعالى عنه and Hadhrat Husain رضي الله تعالى عنه whilst looking at them. "O Allaah I love them, I ask you to also show love towards them." *(Thirmizi)*

Once whilst **walking along with Hadhrat Hasan** رضى الله تعالى عنه **on his blessed shoulders**, Nabi ﷺ made the following dua, "O Allaah I love him, and ask You to love him also." *(Thirmizi)*

This is how Nabi ﷺ would sometimes play with Hadhrat Husain رضى الله تعالى عنه:

Imam Muslim narrates the following incident in his compilation of Muslim Shareef.

The Sahaba رضى الله تعالى عنه once saw **Nabi ﷺ lifting Hadhrat Husain رضى الله تعالى عنه at the shoulders** and smilingly saying to him, "Climb higher, climb higher." Until his feet were in line with the blessed chest of Nabi ﷺ. He then said to him, "Open your mouth." When Hadhrat Husain رضى الله تعالى عنه opened his mouth, **Nabi ﷺ sucked on his** (Husains' رضى الله تعالى عنه) **tongue then made the following dua for him. "O Allaah** I love him, and I ask you to love him and love all those who have love for him!" *(Sahih Muslim)*

These two (Hadhrat Hasan رضى الله تعالى عنه and Hadhrat Husain رضى الله تعالى عنه) are my flowers in this world:

Under the chapter of the virtues of Sahaba رضى الله تعالى عنه a famous incident narrated by Hadhrat Abu Hurairah رضى الله تعالى عنه is mentioned as follows. He says, "Once Nabi ﷺ was seated on the pulpit delivering a sermon when **he saw Hadhrat Hasan and Hadhrat Husain رضى الله تعالى عنه donned in reddish coloured garments stumbling and walking**

around. He descended from the pulpit and went to them. **He then carried them and went back to the pulpit placing them before him.** He then said, "'Allaah has correctly stated that your wealth and children are both tests for you. I saw these children stumbling before me and I could not bare this. I therefore got off the pulpit in between the sermon and picked them up."' *(Thirmizi)*

Nabi ﷺ is also reported to have said, "These two are my flowers in this world." *(Bukhari)*

Whenever Nabi ﷺ would visit Hadhrat Fatima رضى الله تعالى عنها he would say, "Bring my sons to me." When Hadhrat Hasan and Hadhrat Husain رضى الله تعالى عنه would come to him, **he would smell them then hug them holding them close to his bosom.** *(Thirmizi)*

Nabi ﷺ is reported to have said, "Hadhrat Hasan and Hadhrat Husain رضى الله تعالى عنه would be the leaders of the youngsters in paradise." *(Thirmizi)*

Chapter 2

Love shown towards children in general:

Love shown towards a little girl who lost some money:

Nabi ﷺ was once on his way when he saw a young girl along the road. This young girl was crying. He asked her as to why she was crying, to which she said that her master had sent her to purchase flour, but she had mislaid the money he had given her. **Nabi ﷺ gave her money to buy the flour, but she was still crying.** Upon asking why she was still crying, she said that her master would be angry at her (for taking so long). **Nabi ﷺ now showed her even more love and accompanied her to her master. When they reached her master, he asked the master to over look her mistake and show kindness towards her.** He then returned from there.

Love shown towards three little children playing merrily:

Once while passing by three children who were out playing Nabi ﷺ indicated towards one of them and **lifted him onto his mount seating the child in front of him.** He then **lifted the second child and seated him behind himself on the mount.** Now there remained no place on the mount so he **placed his hand on the head of the third child and prayed for him. He did this thrice.** *(Musnad-e-Ahmed)* This third child was the child of Hadhrat Jafar رَضِىَاللهُتَعَالَىَعَنْهُ.

Look at the affection shown towards these little children. He pleased the first by seating the child before him on the same mount, the second by seating him behind him on the same mount and he prayed three times for third **whilst smiling at him** and in this way pleased the third child as well. May Almighty Allaah send thousands of salutations and peace upon His Beloved Muhammed ﷺ.

The fortunate child from Yamaamah:

On the occasion of the Hajj of Nabi ﷺ which is referred to as the farewell hajj, a new born child was brought to Nabi ﷺ. **This child was born that very same day. Nabi ﷺ asked the child, "Who am I?" This one day old child spoke and replied, "You are Rasul-the messenger of Allaah!"** Nabi ﷺ said, "You have indeed spoken the truth. May Allaah shower you with His blessings." As a result of this incident, people referred to that child as "Mubarakul-Yamaamah."

(Due to this miracle (of Nabi ﷺ) this child was given the power to utter that single statement only and never spoke again until he reached the normal age of speech.)

A fortunate child who received the benediction of Nabi ﷺ:

Imam Bukhari رَحْمَةُاللهِتَعَالَى narrates from Hadhrat Saad Saaidi رَضِىَاللهُتَعَالَىَعَنْهُ that a utensil with some form of drink was presented to Nabi ﷺ. On this occasion, a young Sahabi (Hadhrat Ibn Abbaas رضي الله تعالى عنه) was seated to the right of Nabi ﷺ whilst senior Sahaba the likes of Abu Bakr رضي الله تعالى عنه were seated to his left. After having drunk of this particular drink (as was the habit of Nabi ﷺ when something needed to be distributed he would begin with those to his right) he, keeping this principle in mind, asked the youngster, **"Would you permit me to begin on my left with these elderly people seated to my left and give them to drink my left over of the drink?"** The child responded thus, "I will never give preference to anyone over myself when it comes to my share of your left over's, O Rasul- the messenger of Allaah ﷺ!" *(Bukhari)*

We salute the intelligence, understanding and foresight of this young child...........! The senior Sahaba رضي الله تعالى عنه themselves were outstanding, but what to say of their children?! All praise be to Allaah, indeed they are worthy of being envied. We pray that Allaah grant our elders even a slight resemblance to the elders amongst the Sahaba رضي الله تعالى عنه and our children a slight resemblance to their children, this is something we desperately need in this day and age.

A request by
Hadhrat Abu Hurairah رضي الله تعالى عنه
from Nabi ﷺ to make dua
for the guidance of his mother
towards Islaam:

Hadhrat Abu Hurairah رضي الله تعالى عنه accepted Islaam at the hands of Nabi ﷺ and become a Sahabi worthy of being envied. His mother though, detested Islaam. Whenever he left the gathering of Nabi ﷺ to return home, his mother would rebuke him and say evil things to him. He on the other hand was eager that she accepts Islaam. He therefore always told his mother about the beauties of Islaam, but to no avail.

He finally came to Nabi ﷺ and said;
"I am desirous of my mothers accepting Islaam, but she persists on her refusal to do so. O Nabi ﷺ, please make dua unto Allaah that He guides her to Islaam."

Nabi ﷺ immediately made dua for her!

Upon returning home he found that his mother had bolted the door from the inside. She then called out, "O Abu Hurairah, I have accepted Islaam!"

He then went back to Nabi ﷺ and gave him the glad tidings of her accepting Islaam and he asked Nabi ﷺ to make dua for his mother and himself. **Nabi ﷺ then made dua that Allaah make him and his mother beloved to all the believers!** Abu Hurairah رضي الله تعالى عنه used to later say that it was as a result of the dua of Nabi ﷺ that anybody who heard his name would love him!

Allaah forbid, if any person's parents are deprived of Imaan or lack in good deeds, seeking dua from the pious for their guidance is in following with the Sunnat of the Sahaba رضي الله تعالى عنهم. We should therefore do so.

A child cries, "O Allaah send down revelation in support of me!"

Hadhrat Umair Ibn Saad Ansaari رضي الله تعالى عنه was not yet able to stand upright when he was orphaned. The father had neither left any wealth behind which could have been of assistance to this young boy and his mother. After some time, his mother remarried a man from the Aus tribe by the name of Jallaas Ibn Suwaid. Jallaas took this child also into his care. **Within a few months or years, the kindness and affection of Jallaas caused this child to even forget that he had lost his biological father.**

Now Umair ﵁ would often go to the Masjid and be honoured to witness the noble countenance and refined character of Nabi ﷺ. At a very young age he was blessed with the honour of having performed salah behind Nabi ﷺ. His mother used to be very happy to see him frequenting the Masjid. While life was carrying on smoothly in this manner, a great test over came this young boy. Perhaps very few are tested at such an age. Details are as follows..........

In the 9ᵗʰ year after migration, Nabi ﷺ intended engaging in battle with the Romans at a place called Tabook. He therefore commanded the Muslims to prepare themselves. Despite the intense heat and the orchards ready for harvest, the Muslims began all out preparations. The hypocrites found it very difficult to strive under such conditions and thus, begun to put doubts in the hearts and minds of the believers. Nevertheless the Muslim army was prepared.

Hadhrat Umair ﵁ watched the Sahaba ﵃ bringing provisions, weapons etc. and presenting these to Nabi ﷺ. The Ansaari women even brought forth their jewellery, clothes and other items. Seeing this he became very elated and he desired that his father similarly assisted financially and even physically participate in this battle.

He would come home and mention what he had seen to **his father.** But, to no avail. As an encouragement for his father, he would narrate how he had seen the Sahaba ﵃ bringing forth whatever they could and presenting these to Nabi ﷺ. When the self esteem of his father could no longer contain this, he said a few bitter words. He **said, "If Muhammed ﷺ is true in his claim of Nabuwaat-prophethood, we are worse than donkeys!"**

Hearing these bitter words, Umair رضى الله تعالى عنه began to think. It seems my father has been influenced by the hypocrites. Should I keep this a secret or be a true servant of Islaam and reveal this to Nabi ﷺ? He finally chose to give preference to the love of Nabi ﷺ and Islaam over the love for his father. **He then came and narrated the entire incident to Nabi ﷺ who sent for his father.** When asked, his father denied any such statement. The Sahaba رضى الله تعالى عنهم were absolutely amazed, whilst the hypocrites sided with their comrade and swore oaths that it was impossible for him to have said something of that nature. They said that he was definitely speaking the truth, and the young boy is lying.

Now this young Umair رضى الله تعالى عنه began to cry saying in his heart, "O Allaah, you are well aware that I have spoken the truth, please send down revelation as testimony on my behalf."

In due cause revelation began to descend upon Nabi ﷺ and the Sahaba رضى الله تعالى عنهم realised this.

Each one of them remained seated in his place and had his gaze fixed on Nabi ﷺ. Seeing this, signs of fear appeared on the face of Jallaas while signs of joy appeared on the face of Hadhrat Umair رضى الله تعالى عنه.

Once the revelation had come to completion, Nabi ﷺ read the verses which when translated are as follows, "They take oaths that they had not uttered such statements whereas indeed they had uttered these statements of disbelief. They had indeed to do that which they were

unable to do. Their anger (within) is as a result of Allaah
and his Rasul ﷺ having made them (Sahaba رضى الله تعالى عنهم)
independent by their grace. If they turn in repentance it
would be better for them, and if they do not repent then
certainly Allaah will inflict upon them a painful
punishment in this world and in the Akhiraat-hereafter.
They will then not find any ally or assistant on the surface
of this earth." *(Surah Toubah v.74)*

Jallaas hearing this began shivering and crying saying,
"O Rasulullaah ﷺ I repent, O Rasulullaah ﷺ I repent.
Verily Umair رضى الله تعالى عنه had spoken the truth and I was the
liar. O Rasulullaah ﷺ please ask Allaah to accept my
repentance." He then became a sincere Muslim- رضى الله تعالى عنه.

**Rasulullaah ﷺ then turned to Umair رضى الله تعالى عنه and
in a tone of congratulating him, very affectionately
holding him by the ear said, "My dear, these ears had
heard correctly and Allaah has given testimony to it."**

Thereafter, whenever Umair رضى الله تعالى عنه was mentioned in
the presence of his father Jallaas رضى الله تعالى عنه, he would say,
"This child has indeed saved me from disbelief and freed
my neck from Jahannam."

Nabi's ﷺ shedding tears
at the demise of a child:

Hadhrat Anas رضى الله تعالى عنه narrates that he accompanied
Nabi ﷺ to a certain tribe. An Ansaari woman sent a
message to Nabi ﷺ that her child was in the throws of
death and he should avail himself. Nabi ﷺ immediately
proceeded to her house together with his companions.
Upon taking the child into his lap, the child breathed its

last. The blessed eyes of Rasulullaah ﷺ began to flow with tears.

The mother then said, "Allaah has taken back his trust from his servant. Everything that remains also belongs to him and everything has an appointed time. I will therefore exercise patience and reap the rewards thereof."

Nabi ﷺ then said, "There is a lofty abode in paradise which cannot be acquired through neither salah, fasting or any other act of virtue." He was asked as to how it could then be acquired. He said, "By exercising patience when afflicted by a calamity."

Nabi's ﷺ crying with the daughter of Hadhrat Zaid رضي الله تعالى عنه:

Hadhrat Khalid Ibn Shumair رضي الله تعالى عنه narrates that when Hadhrat Zaid رضي الله تعالى عنه was martyred in the battle of Muta, Nabi ﷺ proceeded to his house. **Upon seeing Nabi ﷺ the daughter of Hadhrat Zaid رضي الله تعالى عنه began to cry. While consoling her, Nabi ﷺ was also crying.**

Seeing this, Hadhrat Saad Ibn Ubaadah رضي الله تعالى عنه asked, "What is this O Nabi ﷺ? Why are you crying so profusely?"

Nabi ﷺ replied, "This is a friend crying in memory of his friend." (In other words, in memory of his beloved companion Hadhrat Zaid رضي الله تعالى عنه, he could not contain himself but shed a few tears.)

The affection of Nabi ﷺ towards the father of Hadhrat Aasim رضي الله تعالى عنه:

Aasim's رضي الله تعالى عنه father's name was Qatadah Ibn N'umaan رضي الله تعالى عنه who had fought alongside Nabi ﷺ in the battle of Uhud with great valour.

Aasim says that his father told him that during the battle an arrow had struck him in the eye causing the eye to fall out of its socket onto his cheek. People told him that the eye will have to be severed, but Nabi ﷺ felt otherwise. **He then called for him and took the hanging eye into his blessed hand passing his hand over it and caressing it.** He then made dua that Allaah should bless this eye with beauty (and thereafter replaced the eye into its socket!) Anyone who ever met him thereafter could never tell that one of his eyes had ever been injured! *(Bukhari/Muslim)*

(In a narration of Baihaqi it has been mentioned that the eye which was miraculously cured was the more beautiful eye of the two.)

A little girl who played with the seal of Nabuwaat-Prophethood:

The Daughter of Khalid Ibn Saeed ﷺ once came to the gathering of Nabi ﷺ. She herself narrates that she was a little girl when she had once come to the gathering wearing a yellowish colour garment. Upon seeing it Nabi ﷺ remarked, "Sanah, sanah!" which is the equivalent of, wow that's beautiful, in the Abyssinian language.

She says that her father sat himself in the gathering whilst she began to play with seal of Nabuwaat-Prophethood on the back of Nabi ﷺ between his shoulder blades. (This was a piece of flesh the size of a pigeon's egg which protruded between the shoulder blades of Nabi ﷺ and is referred to as the seal of Nabuwaat-Prophethood.)

After some time when her father had noticed her playing with this, he tried to move her away and reprimanded her. **Nabi ﷺ told him to leave her and let her be.** He then made the following dua which is to be read at the time of donning a new garment. Go on wearing it until it is worn out. He repeated these words thrice.

She says that in this state of ecstasy of having the dua of Nabi ﷺ she went on holding this seal and kissing it playing with it! Subhaanallaah! What an enviable little child! *(Bukhari)*

There was yet another seal of Nabuwaat-Prophethood which was totally different from the one mentioned above. This was specifically made because the Sahaba رضي الله تعالى عنهم had told Nabi ﷺ that he sends letters of invitation to Islaam to the kings of various places whereas these kings do not accept or even read letters which do not have a stamp on it. Therefore for the fulfilment of this objective, Nabi ﷺ had had a ring made with the inscription Muhammadur-Rasulullah on it, which was stamped on letters sent out.

Would this woman fling her child into a fire?

The second caliph of our beloved Nabi ﷺ, Hadhrat Umar رضي الله تعالى عنه narrates an amazing incident which had taken place during the life of Nabi ﷺ.

He says:
A few slaves from the Hawaazin tribe had come into the possession of Nabi ﷺ. Amongst them was a woman, who whenever she saw a child, would take the child and holding it to her bosom wish to feed the child. She would also say, "Alas my child, alas my child!" (In reality this woman had lost her child.)

Nabi ﷺ then asked, "Do you people think that this woman would ever fling her child into the fire?" We said that she would never do so. Nabi ﷺ then said, "Allaah is indeed more compassionate towards his servants than this woman towards her child!" *(Bukhari – Kitaabul-Aadaab)*

Beloved children, when our Creator is so compassionate towards us, why do we not obey his commands and thereby make our earthly life a living paradise? Why do we not sacrifice everything to earn His pleasure? Undoubtedly He would then reward us with tremendous rewards and become pleased with us.

Nabi ﷺ gives a little child a fruit:

Whenever the companions of Nabi ﷺ came across the first fruit of the season, they would present it to Nabi ﷺ.

On seeing it he would recite the following dua, "O Allaah grant us blessings in our fruit, grant us blessings in our city and grant us blessings in both our large measures and small measures of weight. O Allaah verily Ibrahim ﷺ was your servant, Rasul-messenger and friend. He prayed to you to bless the land of Makkah. O Allaah I am also your servant and Rasul-messenger, I also ask you to bless Madeenah and increase its blessings."

He would then call the youngest child in the gathering and present the fruit to that child. *(Muslim Shareef Kitaabul-Hajj)*

Beloved children, do you not see the compassion our beloved master displayed towards children? All praise is to Allaah. Indeed we have a most compassionate master. May Almighty Allaah keep showering him with thousands of salutations.

Our beloved Nabi ﷺ greeting little children:

I will now narrate another incident which you will be pleased to read. Perhaps you might be encouraged to practice and thereby become a practical example for other.

Hadhrat Sh'uba رحمه الله تعالى narrates that he was once walking with his mentor Thabit Bunaani r.a when they passed by a group of children. Upon passing them he greeted these little children then said that he was once walking with his mentor Hadhrat Anas رضي الله تعالى عنه when they passed upon a group of children and he also greeted them. **He then said that he was once walking with his master Hadhrat Muhammed ﷺ when they passed by some children. When passing the children Nabi ﷺ greeted them.** *(Thirmizi)*

What lesson have you learnt by reading this Hadith? Ponder a little, and then answer. I am sure you have learnt of the compassion which Nabi ﷺ had for children.........
but together with that I am certain you have also noticed how **all the personalities** mentioned in the above incident **practiced precisely as their mentors did.** Another lesson which we could derive from this incident is that **our predecessors used every opportunity to impart knowledge, whether whilst walking or stationary.** This is how good spread. These days with the exception of a few the majority are involved in the spreading of evils, and this is why we find the disobedience of Allaah widespread. If only we could look into our past and use it to brighten our future thus bringing alive good morals and character.

Assalaamu alaikum O children:

Like the above mentioned narration, the following few narrations are also regarding greeting of children. These narrations teach us that adults should (not feel it bellow themselves) to initiate greeting children. Similarly children should also greet one another.

It has been narrated that Nabi ﷺ told Hadhrat Anas رضي الله تعالى عنه that he should greet his family members when reaching home as this will be a means of blessings for him and his family. *(Thirmizi vol.3 pg.99)*

A Sahabi narrates he was amongst **a few children who were playing when Nabi ﷺ passed by them and greeted them (first).** *(Ibn Majah Kitabul-Adab)*

Hadhrat Anas Ibn Maalik رضي الله تعالى عنه passed by some children and greeted them saying that Nabi ﷺ used to do the same. *(Bukhari)*

Hadhrat Anas Ibn Maalik رضي الله تعالى عنه says that we were a group of children who were playing about when Nabi ﷺ passed by us and greeted us thus, "Assalaamu alaikum O children!" *(Musnad-e-Ahmed)*

Nabi's ﷺ instruction
not to kill children while at war:

Najdah bin Aamir sent a letter to Hadhrat Ibn Abbaas رضي الله تعالى عنه asking him a few questions.
One of the questions was whether Nabi ﷺ had ever killed children during the battles. **He replied that Nabi ﷺ never instructed the killing of children.** *(Musnad-e-Ahmed)*

A child says, "That's a secret of Nabi ﷺ!"

Hadhrat Anas رضي الله تعالى عنه was honoured to be in the service of Nabi ﷺ for ten years continuously.

He narrates:

One day after attending to Nabi ﷺ I thought that Nabi ﷺ was taking his afternoon nap so I would go out for a while. As I looked out, I found some kids playing outside. I stood by watching them play. A little while later Nabi ﷺ also arrived. Upon arrival he greeted the children then called me and sent me on an errand. He then went towards a shady spot and sat down waiting until I returned.

As I had gone out to fulfil the errand, I ran late on my return home. Upon my return, my mother enquired as to why I was delayed. I said that I had gone on an errand for Nabi ﷺ. She then asked me as regards the errand to which I said I would not disclose the secret of Nabi ﷺ! **My mother then said, "O son, never ever disclose the secrets of Nabi ﷺ.** (*Musnad-e-Ahmed, Muslim*)

Dear children, have you pondered over this incident? This intelligent young child did not expose the secret of Nabi ﷺ to his mother even. Coupled with this, after having been trained and mentored in the blessed company of Nabi ﷺ, he has also thought us that although our parents deserve the utmost respect; this respect will never supersede the respect of Nabi ﷺ. Therefore, the commands of Nabi ﷺ will always be given preference over that of our parents'.

Nabi's ﷺ kindness towards Hadhrat Ali رضى الله تعالى عنه:

Dear children, you should know who was the first amongst the children to accept Islaam? Who was the first child to embrace Islaam? It was none other than Ali رضى الله تعالى عنه.

Abu Talib who was the father of Ali ﷺ was experiencing financial difficulties due to a severe drought. For this reason, Nabi ﷺ had taken Ali ﷺ into his custody when he was about four or five years old. Nabi ﷺ used to show a lot of kindness towards him. He would take him wherever he went and would seat him beside himself when eating. He inculcated within him good habits.

When the command of Allaah was revealed, that Nabi ﷺ should sound the warning of Allaah, he gathered his family members and presented the invitation of Islaam to them in one gathering. There was not a single person in the entire gathering that accepted the invitation, besides Ali ﷺ, who at the top of his voice proclaimed, **"I maybe young and weak, but I would always support the cause of the true religion!"** It was in this way that Ali ﷺ had become the first child to accept Islaam. *(Al-Isabah)*

Love shown towards the children of a martyr:

Our beloved Nabi ﷺ had a paternal cousin by the name of Jafar ﷺ. He was granted martyrdom in the battle of Muta. After his martyrdom Nabi ﷺ went to his house and called Jafar's ﷺ three sons, O'wn, Muhammed and Abdullah ﷺ. **He then held them to his chest in a most affectionate manner.**

While embracing them affectionately, Nabis' ﷺ eyes were flowing with tears. Seeing his tears their mother asked regarding Jafar's ﷺ well being. Nabi ﷺ then informed her that he had been martyred. Hearing this she began crying most profusely. Nabi ﷺ then took all of them to one his homes and arranged meals for them saying that this was a day of great grief in their lives.

Hadhrat Abdullah Ibn Jafar رضي الله عنه the youngest son says, "Nabi ﷺ took us along to his house and shared his meals with us. **He was also most affectionate towards us (during this time of grief.) We remained his guests for three days.** *(Tabaqat Ibn Saad)*

The effects of the love shown by Nabi ﷺ to Hadhrat Zaid عليه السلام:

Hadhrat Zaid رضي الله عنه was a slave boy gifted to Nabiﷺ by his first wife Hadhrat Khadijah رضي الله عنها. On one occasion Nabi ﷺ took him to the house of Allaah (the Ka'bah) and announced, "Listen well, Zaid is my adopted son!" Now, what was the reason for this announcement? To understand this you would have to read the following incident. So let us read the incident.

Hadhrat Zaid Ibn Haritha رضي الله عنه belongs to the noble tribe of Quzza who hail from Yemen. His mother was from the M'an tribe. At the tender age of eight he was accompanying his mother to parents home. They met up with a group of treacherous riders from the tribe of Banu Qain on the way. The riders had evil intentions whilst mother and son were merrily going along unaware of their intentions. When they came into close proximity of the riders, one of the riders suddenly lifted Zaid رضي الله عنه and went off. His mothers' heart was shattered and she began pleading and begging him to return her child, but the hard hearted man refused to accede. Whilst looking towards them, they finally rode out of sight. Zaid رضي الله عنه was also crying and pleading, but to no avail. His mother forgot all about where she was headed and retuned to her marital home in a terrible state of mind.

Zaids' رضي الله عنه father, Haritha Bin Shurahbeel was also very much grieved on the loss of his son. He exhausted every resource of his in search of his beloved son. He searched every dessert, every jungle, every town, every city, every village, every province, but his efforts were in vain. He never lost hope though and relentlessly continued his search. Every moment of separation only increased his grief.

The Banu Qain rider in the meantime took Zaid رضي الله تعالى عنه to the Ukkaaz Fair. Amongst other things sold at this fair, were slave girls and boys. Zaid رضي الله تعالى عنه was amongst those for sale. Hakim Ibn Hizaam was also present at this fair, and he purchased Zaid رضي الله تعالى عنه for his paternal aunt Khadijah رضي الله تعالى عنها. He then brought him over (to Makkah) and made him over to her.

In this way Zaid رضي الله تعالى عنه came into the possession of the wealthiest of businesswoman and widow of Makkah. When she married Nabi ﷺ, she made presented Zaid ﷺ as a gift unto Nabi ﷺ. **Now Zaid رضي الله تعالى عنه became one of those fortunate enough to be in the slavery of the mercy of both worlds. This was something predestined. Outwardly his incident of being taken captive is indeed a sad incident, but who would have ever thought what goodness his destiny had in store for him?** In that he was to be honoured as a servant of none other than Rasulullaah ﷺ! Here he was to be in his service day and night, and thus count his soul from amongst the dwellers of Jannat!

Time flew by. On the occasion of Hajj some years later, a few folks from the tribe of Banu Kalb had come to Makkah intending to perform Hajj. They immediately srecognized this child who had been taken away from his parents and narrated to him his father Harithas' grieving over him. **When Hadhrat Zaid رضي الله تعالى عنه heard of his fathers' grief, he said a few couplets to console his father and asked the members of Banu Kalb to convey them to his father.**

When his father learnt that his son was alive, he was overtaken by joy and wished he could grow wings and fly to Makkah and receive his son. He took his brother Ka'b along with him and set out on the road to Makkah as quick as he could.

Upon reaching Makkah they came into the noble presence of Nabi ﷺ and presented their case thus, "O son of Abdullah! O the member of Banu Haashim! O the leader of his people! We have come to you regarding the matter of a piece of our hearts and flesh which is in your possession. Please accept a ransom from us and show kindness towards us." Nabi ﷺ asked, "And what would that be?" They said, "Zaid Ibn Haritha رضي الله تعالى عنه." Nabi ﷺ listened attentively that shook the heavens! **He said that they should give Zaid ؓ a choice. Should he choose them; he will make him over without any ransom!** On the contrary, if he chose Nabi ﷺ; then, by Allaah, he would not hand him to someone else when he has chosen Nabi ﷺ himself. Hearing this, Haritha Bin Shurahbeel said, **"You have given us more than what we had bargained for! You have indeed been fair and kind to us."**

In the meantime Zaid رضي الله تعالى عنه was called and asked, "Do you recognise these people?" He said, "Yes, this is my father Haritha, and that is my uncle Ka'b." Nabi ﷺ then said to him, "They have come to fetch you. You have a choice, you can either stay with me or go back with them." The ears of history now heard the most unique answer. **He said, "O Rasulullaah ﷺ you are indeed my mother and father! I will never give preference to anyone over you!"**

The father and uncle were shocked out of their wits and could not believe their ears! That Zaid رضي الله تعالى عنه had preferred slavery over freedom! (Yes, but they were ignorant and unacquainted with the honour in this slavery!)

Therefore they said, "Do you prefer to remain a slave and leave your freedom, father, uncle and family?" Love had now surpassed the boundaries of the test. Zaid رضى الله تعالى عنه answered thus, **"Yes, the being of my master is such, that I cannot give preference to anyone over him! The enjoyment of being in his slavery is more treasured than thousands of freedom!"**

Dear children, when Hadhrat Zaid رضى الله تعالى عنه had given preference to Nabi ﷺ over his father and uncle, do you not think Nabi ﷺ was of a noble personality? It was for this reason that he had taken him to the Ka'bah and announced that Zaid رضى الله تعالى عنه was his son and in future he should be referred to as his son. All praise is for Allaah, Zaid رضى الله تعالى عنه fulfilled the rights of expressing love, and with what love did not Nabi ﷺ refer to him as his own?

Nabi ﷺ carries a new born baby in his lap:

The attendant of Nabi ﷺ, Hadhrat Anas رضى الله تعالى عنه brought his new born brother to Nabi ﷺ and he **took the child into his lap with great love and affection.** He then asked Anas رضى الله تعالى عنه "Do you have any dates with you?" Anas رضى الله تعالى عنه said that he did have dates with him. **He then took the dates and chewed in it after which he placed it in the mouth of the new born child** who immediately began to suck on it with great relish. (What a fortunate child! Indeed very enviable!) Seeing this Nabi ﷺ jokingly said, "Look at how the Ansaar love their dates!" *(Muslim Kitabul-Adab)*

The first thing a fortunate child suckles on is the saliva of Nabi ﷺ:

Hadhrat Asmaa Bint Abu Bakr رضى الله تعالى عنها was the first woman to give birth after migration. She had given

birth at Quba. Nabi ﷺ named this child Abdullaah. The believers and more especially, those who had migrated were elated as it had become common that the Jews had cast a spell over the Muslims and therefore they could not bare any offspring.

When he was born, he was brought to Nabi ﷺ who took him into his noble lap then put some of his blessed saliva into his mouth! He then chewed on some dates which he thereafter put into this fortunate child's mouth to suck on. He also made dua that this child be blessed! (What a fortunate little boy!) *(Bukhari Shareef Kitaabul Aqeeqah)*

In another narration Hadhrat Abu Moosa رضى الله تعالى عنه narrates that he brought one of his new born children to Nabi ﷺ who took the child into his lap, chewed on dates, then placed the dates in the mouth of the child to suckle on. **He even made dua that the child be blessed.** He then made over the child to me. *(Bukhari Shareef Kitaabul Aadaab)*

Being blessed with dignity by virtue of the saliva of Nabi ﷺ:

A child was brought to Nabi ﷺ. Nabi ﷺ chewed on Ajwah dates then placed the dates in this child's mouth. The child immediately began sucking on the dates with much relish. Nabi ﷺ then said, "Look at the passion the Ansaar have for dates!" He then passed his blessed hand over the face of the child and named him Abdullaah. It has been reported that there was no child that had more dignity and prominence than this child amongst the Ansaar! *(Musnad-e-Ahmed)*

Nabi ﷺ advices adults as regards children:

Once while visiting a Sahabi, Nabi ﷺ saw the Sahabi call a child indicating that he intended giving him/her something. Nabi ﷺ seeing this enquired, "What do you intend giving him/her?" He said that he intended giving the child some dates. Nabi ﷺ then said, "Had you not given him/her anything, a sin would have been recorded against your name in your book of deeds!" People pacify children by speaking lies to them, whereas this something questionable in the light of Islaam. *(Abu Dawud Kitaabul-Aadaab)*

On one occasion at battle a few children were killed. When the news reached Nabi ﷺ, he was very grieved. **Someone argued that they were not Muslim children. In spite of this Nabi ﷺ still remained grieved and warned that no child should ever be killed in the future.**

During one battle, whilst giving instructions to the Sahaba ﷺ, Nabi ﷺ instructed them as regards children, that they should under no circumstances ever be killed. *(Muslim Shareef)*

Nabi'ﷺ s advice to a woman mourning her child:

Hadhrat Anas Ibn Maalik ﷺ says that Nabi ﷺ once passed by a woman who was mourning the death of her child. Upon seeing her he said, "Fear Allaah exercise patience." The woman asked, "And how would you know the extent of my grief?"

After advising her, Nabi ﷺ left. Later on the woman was informed that she had in actual fact refused the advice of Nabi ﷺ. No sooner did she hear this, she became afraid and rushed of to Nabi ﷺ. Upon reaching him she found that he had no door keeper (in spite of him being the Nabi of Allaah.) She excused herself saying, "I did not realise that it was you, therefore I had responded in that manner." Nabi ﷺ then told her, "True patience is patience borne at the precise moment of the calamity befalling a person." *(Muslim Shareef Kitaabul-Janaaiz)*

With these words our beloved Nabi ﷺ forgave her and taught her that true patience is the acceptance of the decree of Allaah, remembering him at the time of a calamity, and not lamenting over ones loss.

Nabi ﷺ perceives a beautiful scent on the journey of Mi'raj:

Nabi ﷺ whilst on the journey of Mi'raj perceived a beautiful scent. He asked his companion Jibraeel ﷺ as to where the scent emanated from. He was told that it emanated from the grave of the woman who used to comb the hair of the daughter of (Firoun) Pharaoh.

One day whilst combing the hair of his Pharaohs' daughter, the comb slipped out of her hand. When picking it up she said, Bismillaah. Pharaohs' daughter hearing this said, "My father is your Rabb and you should take his name!" The woman said, "My Rabb and the Rabb of your father is Allaah." The daughter said that she would report the woman to her father informing him that the woman believed in another Rabb.

Upon being informed by his daughter, Pharaoh summoned the woman into his court. He then asked her, "Do you invoke a Rabb other than me?" The woman said, "Yes, your Rabb and my Rabb is none other than Allaah!"

Enraged with her response, Pharaoh ordered that a copper caldron be brought and oil should be boiled in it. When this was done, he ordered that the woman's children be brought and each one should be thrown into the boiling oil before her eyes! **The woman said, "If this is what you have decided, then so be it, but I ask you to gather our bones after we are burnt and bury them in one place". Pharaoh said that this would definitely be done.**

In this way all her children accept for one child who was still suckling and had not reached the age of speaking was left. When this child was about to be thrown, the woman became anxious and perturbed. Allaah granted this child the ability to speak and it said, "O My Mother, do not fear! Dive into this oil! Verily the difficulties of this life as compared to the difficulties of the hereafter are incomparable!" Hearing this she dived into the oil with her child to save her Imaan and in this way earned the pleasure of her Rabb.

Today, because of the great sacrifice of this woman and her children, Allaah has caused a scent to emanate from her grave! *(Musnad-e-Ahmed)*

Dear son, is there any milk for us to drink?

Hadhrat Abdullaah Ibn Masood ﷺ recollects a meeting with Nabi ﷺ during his childhood in the following incident.

He says: I was a shepherd in Makkah and I used to take the goats of the famous Kaafir Uqbah Ibn Abi Mueet out to graze. One day whilst out grazing the goats, Nabi ﷺ and his companion Abu Bakr Siddeeq ﷺ passed by and asked me if I could spare them some milk to drink. I said that there was plenty milk, but the goats were placed in my trust and did not belong to me; therefore I could not give them any milk.

Nabi ﷺ thereupon asked me if there was any goat which was not milk giving. I said there was such a goat. He asked me to bring the goat. When I presented the goat to him, he read something then passed his hand over the teats of the goat. The teats were suddenly laden with milk! Nabi ﷺ then milked the goat, drank of the milk, gave Abu Bakr رضي الله تعالى عنه to drink, and gave me to drink also. He then again read something and passed his hand over the teats of the goat and they returned to their original empty condition!

The status of Nabi ﷺ immediately increased in the eyes of Ibn Masood رضي الله تعالى عنه and he asked Nabi ﷺ to teach him those words. Nabi ﷺ was pleased with Ibn Masood رضي الله تعالى عنه and praised him saying that he was a very intelligent young boy. *(Musnad-e-Ahmed)*

In a very short while thereafter he entered the fold of Islaam and became the famous Ibn Masood رضي الله تعالى عنه.

May Allaah also make us such Muslims whose speech and actions become the means of others guidance and salvation from going astray, Aameen.

Unlimited affection shown towards his special attendant Anas رضي الله تعالى عنه:

Hadhrat Anas رضي الله تعالى عنه was a young boy when he was presented to serve Nabi ﷺ. **He was always shown affection and treated compassionately.** Many incidents have been narrated regarding him. He says that Nabi ﷺ came up to him from the back and holding him by the nape and affectionately said, "It's about time you went and done that which I had sent you for!" Anas رضى الله تعالى عنه replied, "I'm on my way." *(Abu-Dawud)*

He was the special attendant of Nabi ﷺ and remained in his service for ten years. He says that never did Nabi ﷺ say "oof" to him nor did he ever say, "Why have you not done such and such" which was asked of him to do. When any loss or damage was caused by him in the house and someone rebuked him, Nabi ﷺ would tell them to leave him as what was meant to happen had happened.

Aeysha رضى الله تعالى عنها says that Nabi ﷺ never raised his hand on a woman or servant. *(Abu-Dawud)*

Nabi ﷺ always showed affection towards children. He treated them with love and he would often pass his hand over them and make dua for them. Should any child come near him, he would take the child into his lap. He would sometimes feed children with great love. Sometimes he would show tongue at children and in this way make them laugh. While lying down he would sometimes lift children from the sole of his feet and sometimes place them on his chest.

When feeding children he would say words that would encourage them to eat and make them happy.

When many children would be gathered in one place Nabi ﷺ would line them up, and then he himself would sit with his hands spread out saying to them that they should race to him. He would even say that he will give the winner such and such a prize. The children in this way would all run towards him, some tripping over his stomach whilst others over his chest. He would then hug them affectionately.

From all the children he would joke the most with Anas رضي الله تعالى عنه. He would jokingly call him, "O the one with two ears."

When walking along if he came across children he would be the first to greet them and he would lovingly talk to them in an informal manner. **He would laugh and joke with them too.** When returning from a journey if he found any children along the way, he would always put one of them onto his conveyance to ride along with him.

A Sahabi says that he was once walking along when he was a little child. He saw Nabi ﷺ coming along towards him. When they passed one another Nabi ﷺ greeted him first.

From the above narrations we clearly see that being affectionate towards children, joking with them, **being informal with them** and playing with them are not against the tenets of piety or taqwa............in fact this is precisely in accordance with the Sunnat if one makes the intention of doing these as a Sunnat and one will be greatly rewarded for it. Similarly, where we find children being instructed to greet adults, we also find that adults should also greet children with love and affection.

Where did your bird go?

Hadhrat Anas رضي الله تعالى عنه had a younger brother by the name of Abu Umair who had a bird as a pet. Once when visiting his family Nabi ﷺ found him very sad (as his bird had died.) Nabi ﷺ affectionately asked him, **"O Abu Umair, what has happened to Nughair?"** This lifted his spirits and made him happy. *(Abu-Dawud)*

Nabi ﷺ awards a child with his shawl:

It was a hot day and everything was at a stand still, but a young twelve year old boy was least concerned. With sword in his hand he was dashing about clearly in search of something. There was anger written his face and this made his face red. His eyes were searching in every direction.

Suddenly he spots Nabi ﷺ behind a boulder. Nabi ﷺ very affectionately asks him what it that he was in search off was. He answered that he was in search of Nabi ﷺ.

The name of this child was Zubair رضى الله تعالى عنه. His mother was Safiyyah and his father was Awaam رضى الله تعالى عنه. This child was the cousin of Nabi ﷺ.

The incident is as follows. The rumour had spread in Makkah that Nabi ﷺ was captured in one of the mountain passes. This was possible as there were many enemies living in Makkah. Therefore, Zubair رضى الله تعالى عنه who was only twelve at the time grabbed a sword and went out solo in search of Nabi ﷺ. When he found Nabi ﷺ, Nabi ﷺ also asked him as to what would he have done if the rumour was in fact true? **This twelve year old boy said replied that he would have shed so much blood in Makkah that not a life would have been spared and there would have been rivers of blood flowing in Makkah! Hearing this Nabi ﷺ began to laugh and in acknowledgment of his bravery he made over his shawl to him as an award.**

Allaah　was also pleased with his response that he despatched Jibraeel عليه السلام conveying salaams to Nabi ﷺ and Zubair رضى الله تعالى عنه. He also informed him that the reward of every person who would lift a sword in the path of Allaah until the Day of Judgment would be recorded in the books of Zubair رضى الله تعالى عنه also as he was **the first to lift sword in the path of Allaah!**

Dear children, valour and bravery are wonderful qualities which we should inculcate within us. Together with this we should adopt the beloved habits of Nabi ﷺ and protect the Deen of Allaah. Our noble master sought refuge from cowardice and laziness, so too should we seek refuge from these habits.

A horse with wings:

Aeysha ﷺ narrates an incident which had taken place prior to her marriage with Nabi ﷺ when she was a young girl. She says that she was once playing with her friends when Nabi ﷺ came to their house. Upon seeing Nabi ﷺ her friends would run away and only return once he had left. *(Abu-Dawud)*

Another incident has been mentioned when Nabi ﷺ upon returning from a campaign while passing by the house of Aeysha ﷺ noticed her toys in the corner of the house as the veil at the entrance had moved slightly. Amongst the toys he noticed a toy horse which had wings. **He jokingly asked her, "What is this O Aeysha? Since when do horses have wings?" Aeysha ﷺ very fittingly responded, "Have you not heard that the horses of Suleiman عليه السلام had wings?" Hearing this Nabi ﷺ smiled to the extent where his teeth became visible.** *(Abu-Dawud)*

A Sahabiyah names her child Muhammed:

Aeysha ﷺ narrates that a woman came to Nabi ﷺ and informed him that she had given birth to a child whom she named Muhammed and she had also given him the title Abul Qasim but she had later learnt that Nabi ﷺ did not approve of this. Nabi ﷺ told her that anyone who names a child after him should not give the child his title and anyone who gives their child his title should not name their child after him. _(Abu-Dawud)_

Someone calls out Abul-Qasim:

Hadhrat Anas رضى الله تعالى عنه narrates that Nabi ﷺ was come from the direction of the Baq'ee cemetery when someone called out from behind him, "O Abul Qasim!" When Nabi ﷺ turned his attention towards that person, he said that he was calling another Abul Qasim and not Nabi ﷺ. Hearing this Nabi ﷺ said, **"You may name after my name, but do not use my title.'** *(Ibn Majah)*

Majority of the Ulama state that this prohibition was restricted to the lifetime of Nabi ﷺ only and not after his demise.

Nabi ﷺ encouraged keeping the name Muhammed:

Hadhrat Jaabir رضى الله تعالى عنه says that a child was born to one of the Sahaba and he named the child Muhammed. When the people learnt of this they objected to it saying that how could he name his child after Nabi ﷺ. They said that they would not leave him until they take him to Nabi ﷺ and resolve the matter by asking Nabi ﷺ if it was alright to name a child after him. This person came to Nabi ﷺ carrying his child and asked, "I have been blessed with a son whom I have named Muhammed and these people have an objection to this." Nabi ﷺ clarified the matter by saying, "You may name your children after my name, but you may not adopt my title (Abul Qasim) as I am Qasim, the one who distributes the wealth between you." *(Muslim Shareef)*

Many more traditions have been narrated by Jaabir رضى الله تعالى عنه under this chapter showing that Nabi ﷺ had clearly permitted the keeping of his name. The scholars of

Ahaadith have mentioned that this name is a very blessed name and any person who has this name turns out to be one of great qualities and goodness. This is why we find the name Muhammed and Ahmed very often in the books of Ahaadith and the books which mention the names of the chain of narrators.

Blessings in this world and the hereafter by virtue of the name Muhammed:

Hadhrat Shah Waleeullah Muhaddith Dehlawi writes in the famous book of history; Madaarijun Nubuwwah:

Keeping the blessed name of Nabi ﷺ is a source of blessing and benefit and a means of protection both in this world and the hereafter. Hadhrat Anas ﷜ narrates that Nabi ﷺ said, "Two people will be made to stand before Allaah and He would order that they be entered into paradise. Both of them would say, '"O our Rabb, what has made us worthy of paradise? We have no good deed to our name accept that we were hopeful that you would grant us entry into paradise through Your mercy.'" Allaah will then say to them that they should enter paradise for he has taken an oath on his very being that he would not put any person who has the name Ahmed or Muhammed into hell!"

In another narration it has been reported that Allaah informed Nabi ﷺ that he has taken an oath by His honour and majesty that He would not punish that person who is named after him (Muhammed ﷺ).

Similarly it is narrated in the Ahaadith that any home wherein there resides a person by the name of Muhammed will be blessed.

It has also been narrated that any group that assembles to consult one another on any matter, and amongst them is a person by the name of Muhammed, Allaah will most certainly bless them in their endeavour.

It has also been reported that Nabi ﷺ will intercede on behalf of that person who is named Muhammed and ensure his entry into paradise. *(Madaarijun Nubuwwah)*

I would have adorned him with jewellery:

Hadhrat Usamah ﷺ was the son of Zaid Ibn Haritha ﷺ who was the slave of Nabi ﷺ. He was very beloved to Nabi ﷺ and Nabi ﷺ would sometimes clean his nose and mouth with his own cloth. Sometimes out of affection he would say, "If Usamah was a girl, I would have adorned him with jewellery and beautified him in such a way that his there would have been widespread talk of his beauty amongst the Arabs!" *(Thirmizi)*

Do you not see how loving Nabi ﷺ was towards children? He was kind and gentle towards little girls also. Look at how lovingly he spoke of Usamah ﷺ. May Allaah reward Nabi ﷺ on behalf of us and send down his unlimited mercy upon him, Aameen.

Affection towards the young:

Nabi ﷺ once said, **"He who does not show mercy to our children and show respect to our elders is not from amongst us."**

On one occasion Nabi ﷺ kissed Hadhrat Hasan ﷺ on his lips while expressing his love to him. A person seeing this said that he had ten children but never displayed such affection towards any of them. Nabi ﷺ responded by saying that he who does not show mercy to others will not be shown mercy by Allaah. *(Muslim Shareef)*

Indeed it is the rights of children that they are shown love and affection, but their foremost rights are that they are given the right upbringing and (Islaamic) education. **Love and affection are shown to a large extent by many, but generally Islaamic education and proper upbringing lacks.** May Allaah grant us the ability to fulfil his rights and the rights of His servants, Aameen.

Hearing the crying of children...

Anas رضى الله تعالى عنه narrates that Nabi ﷺ has said, "I sometimes begin my salah intending to lengthen my salah, **but I shorten my salah when I hear the crying of children as I am aware of what might be going through the hearts of the mothers of the crying children.**" *(Bukhari and Muslim Shareef)*

Our master showed more affection to children than their own mothers and Allaah shows seventy times more mercy to his servants than their mothers show them.

A person who takes care of an orphan child:

Hadhrat Suhail Ibn Saad رضى الله تعالى عنه narrates that Nabi ﷺ said, "**The person who takes care of an orphan child and I will be as close as these two fingers in Jannat.**" (He indicated by raising his index and middle fingers.) *(Bukhari Shareef)*

It has been narrated in another Hadith that Nabi ﷺ has said:

The best of Muslim homes is that home wherein an orphan is taken care of and shown kindness to and the worst of Muslim homes is that home wherein an orphan is ill-treated. *(Ibn Majah)*

Nabi ﷺ is reported to have said that the one who passes his hand over the head of an orphan for the pleasure of Allaah will receive a reward for every strand of hair on the head of the child. He who takes care of an orphan child will be as close as these two fingers to me in Jannat. (Indicating to their closeness by means of his index and middle fingers.) *(Musnad-e-Ahmed)*

Our beloved master showed great love and affection towards children in general, but the love he showed to an orphan child is unimaginable. This is greatly due to the fact that he was an orphan himself. Therefore he devoted special attention towards them and encouraged taking care of them. Secondly, since an orphan has no shoulder to lean on, Islaam and the Quran stress on showing love, taking care and keeping happy an orphan child.

Look for a youngster who will be able to serve me:

Abdullah Ibn Hantab says on the authority of Anas رضي الله تعالى عنه that Nabi ﷺ asked Abu Talha to bring such a young child to him who would be able to serve him. So, Abu Talha رضي الله تعالى عنه put him (Anas رضي الله تعالى عنه) behind him on his conveyance and proceeded to Nabi ﷺ. Anas رضي الله تعالى عنه says that in this way he served Nabi ﷺ until the battle of Khaibar. Whenever Nabi ﷺ would halt at any place he would read the following dua;

"Allaahuma inni a'uzhu bika minal hummi wal huzni wal ajzi wal kasli wal bukhli wal jubni wa dhal'id dayni wa ghalabatir-rijaali."

Translation: "O Allaah I seek refuge in You from all forms of worries and grief and from weakness and laziness and from miserliness and cowardliness and from being overwhelmed by debts and being overpowered by people." *(Bukhari Shareef)*

Her child was with her:

Hadhrat Anas Ibn Maalik رضي الله تعالى عنه narrates that a woman came along with her child to Nabi ﷺ. After engaging in some conversation with Nabi ﷺ he began to praise her and said, "The Ansaar are beloved to me, but you are twice as beloved." *(Bukhari Shareef)*

Beloved children, those who migrated from Makkah to Madeenah with Nabi ﷺ were indeed very beloved to him due to their sacrifices and firm Imaan. As for those who resided in Madeenah, the Ansaar, they were beloved to him for they gave preference to him and showed more love to him than their wealth, family, tribes and honour. Above all, they followed him in total.

You will receive the reward of this child's Hajj:

Hadhrat Ibn Abbaas رضي الله تعالى عنه says that during the days of Hajj Nabi ﷺ passed by a woman who veiled herself with a shawl. Along with her was a young child of approximately eight to ten years of age. She asked Nabiﷺ, "Is there Hajj on this child?" He replied, "Yes, and the reward will be yours."

We learn from this that a child who has reached the age of understanding and is present in the places of hajj with his/her parents, he/she should observe the rituals of Hajj. *(Nasai)*

My child cannot speak:

After having completed the rituals of Hajj on the day Adha while returning Nabi ﷺ passed by a woman who came to him and said, **"This is my child and I have no one else in this world besides him. He has a sickness whereby he is unable to speak."** Nabi ﷺ requested that water be brought to him. When this was brought, he washed both his hands and gargled. He then asked her to give the child some of the water to drink and she should pass the rest of the water over his body. It is hoped that Allaah will cure him.

Hadhrat Umme Jundub ﵂ who was present at the time and is the narrator of this incident, **asked the lady to give her some of the blessed water. The woman refused, saying it was exclusively for the sick child.**

After a year Umme Jundub ﵂ met the woman and asked her as to how the child was doing. She said that the child had been cured and has even excelled other children! *(Ibn Majah)*

Indeed the child's complete recovery and excelling other children was by virtue of the sheer grace of Allaah and the blessings of Nabi ﷺ.

A small child stands in the path of Nabi ﷺ and his companions' ﵃:

Anas Ibn Maalik ﵁ reports that a small child was standing in the centre of the road/pathway which Nabi ﷺ and his companions' were travelling on. The mother of the child seeing this feared that her child would be crushed by them ran frantically towards her child crying out, "My child! My piece of flesh!"

The Sahaba ﷺ witnessing this remarked, "This woman can never fling her child into a fire!" Upon hearing this, Nabi ﷺ, **"Allaah will also not fling his beloved servants into the fire!"** *(Musnad-e-Ahmed)*

Why do you people put your children through difficulty?

Nabi ﷺ once came to Umme Salamah ﷺ. He found a woman present there with her child. The child was bleeding in the throat region. Nabi ﷺ enquired as to what was wrong with the child. He was informed that the child was hurt. He then asked, "Why do you people put your children through such difficulty? Why do you not give the child *Qust-e-Hindi*? Add water to *Qust-e-Hindi* and mix well. Thereafter apply the paste on the child's throat." This was done for the child and the child was cured.

Nabi ﷺ made him sit in front of himself on the same camel:

Ya'laa Ibn Murrah ﷺ has narrated three incidents which he witnessed whilst in the company of Nabi ﷺ in a single lengthy narration. One of the incidents is recorded hereunder as it relates to children and makes good reading for them.

He says that they were once travelling with Nabi ﷺ when they passed by a woman sitting with her child. She came to Nabi ﷺ requesting him to advise her as regards her child who was ill and due to the child's illness the family was undergoing much difficulty. Nabi ﷺ asked

her to hand the child to him. He then took the child and sat
the child before him on the same conveyance. There
remained nothing between him and the child accept for the
stick of the saddle on the camel. Nabi ﷺ then recited the
following dua, "Bismillaahi ana Abdullah. Ikhsa anna
aduwallah." I take the name of Allaah. I am the servant of
Allaah. O the enemy of Allaah, distance yourself from here.
**He then blew into the mouth of the child and returned
the child to the mother. He also told her that she should
inform him about the child on his return.**

The narrator says that when we returned that way,
Nabiﷺ enquired about the well being of the child. The
mother said that from that time on the child never suffered
from the illness. She then brought three goats to us from
which Nabi ﷺ ordered us to take one between those for
travelling. We then moved on ahead. *(Musnad-e-Ahmed)*

Yes, my father is here, he is eating:

Hadhrat Abu Qatadah ﷺ had given a loan to
another Muslim. Due to this person suffering from extreme
poverty, he was unable to repay the debt. Every time Abu
Qatadah ﷺ would come to him seeking the
repayment, he would hide in his house.

One day Abu Qatadah ﷺ came to his house
seeking the repayment. He was inside the house eating at
the time. When Abu Qatadah ﷺ knocked at the door,
this person's child came to the door to find out who was it
and what was it they wanted. Abu Qatadah ﷺ
enquired of the child if his/her father was present. The child
said that he was present, and he was busy eating. Abu
Qatadah then called out to the person saying that he knew
that he was in the house, and that he should please come
out. When the person came out, Abu Qatadah ﷺ

asked him as to why he was in hiding. **The man said that he was undergoing difficult financial conditions. Hearing that he was suffering from poverty, Abu Qatadah** رضي الله تعالى عنه **began crying. He then said, "I have learnt from the king of both worlds that he who gives respite or overlooks the debt of a debtor, Allaah will protect him from the fears and torment of the Day of Judgment." Saying this he forgave his debtor!** (Ahmed)

Let us ponder for a while. **The result of the truth spoken by the child was that the debt of the father was forgiven.** Indeed this is the blessing of speaking the truth. On the other hand, look at the Sahabi; he wipes out the entire debt by virtue of hearing one statement of Nabi ﷺ. He fulfilled the right of the statement of Nabi ﷺ and with what perfection did he enact his teachings?

Nabi ﷺ hears the crying of a child:

Urawa Ibn Zubair رضي الله تعالى عنه narrates that Nabi ﷺ once entered the house of Umme Salamah رضي الله تعالى عنها and heard the sound of a child crying. He asked them, "Are you people not going to the **treat the child for the evil glances that have cast a spell over him/her?**" (i.e. In accordance with the teachings of Islaam the child should definitely should be treated.) *(Muwatta Imam Maalik)*

We learn from various Ahaadith that the evil glance most certainly has an effect on the person whom the glance is cast upon. Therefore the advice of Ulama should be sought and necessary steps within the limits of Shariah should be taken.

Nabi ﷺ visits my father:

Abdullaah Ibn Busr رضي الله تعالى عنه narrates that Nabi ﷺ once visited his father. His father brought *hais* (a type of food made from melted butter, flour and dates) and some water. He presented both these to Nabi ﷺ. Nabi ﷺ drank from the water and made over the remainder to the person seated to his right.

Nabi ﷺ thereafter partook of the dates. I watched as he flicked the pips of the date with the index and middle finger of the left hand out of the plate in which the dates were. When Nabi ﷺ stood up to leave my father also got up with him and requested that he made dua for us. Nabi ﷺ then made dua in the following words, *"Allaahuma baärik lahum fee maa razaqtahum wag fir lahum warhamhum."* Translation: "O Allaah grant them blessings in their sustenance, forgive them and show mercy on them." *(Abu-Dawud)*

Daughters are a shield from the fire of jahannam (hell):

A woman once came begging to the door of Ummul Mu'mineen Hadhrat Aeysha ﷺ accompanied by her two young daughters. At that particular time, there was nothing but a single date in the palace of the king of both worlds! Hadhrat Aeysha ﷺ gave this one date to her.

The motherliness of a mother in her could not allow herself to eat the whole date or even half of it while her children look on. **She therefore broke it into two and gave each child half while she remained hungry!** Aeysha ﷺ was astonished at the love this poor mother had displayed towards her children. When Nabi ﷺ arrived, she narrated the entire incident to him.

Hearing this Nabi ﷺ said, "When a person is given daughters and is tested by means of them, but he/she shows kindness to them, these daughters will become a shield from the fire of jahannam for such a person." *(Muslim)*

A wonderful reward for nurturing two girls:

Nabi ﷺ explaining the revelation regarding the upbringing of two girls explains:

Any person who nurtures and brings up two girls until they reach the age whereby they are able to differentiate (between right and wrong) will have the honour of being this close to me on the Day of Judgement. (Raising his hand whilst keeping together two fingers indicating the closeness.) *(Muslim)*

Can anyone imagine this honour? On another occasion he said that a fathers teaching his a child some good manners, **is better than giving approximately three kilograms towards charity. On another occasion he said that no person can give his child any better gift than sound (deeni) education.** *(Thirmizi)*

Similarly he has mentioned regarding not giving preference to boys over girls that; he who is blessed with a daughter and he spares her life, does not undermine her nor give preference to his sons over her, shall enter jannat. *(Sunan Abu-Dawud)*

A man asks Nabi ﷺ to be a witness to him handing over a slave to his son:

A Sahabi had gifted a slave to one of his sons and he desired that Nabi ﷺ be witness to this act. By and by he comes to Nabi ﷺ and expresses his desire.

Nabi ﷺ asked him whether he had gifted all his children in a like manner. The man said he did not do so. Nabi ﷺ then said, "I will not be a witness to such an unfair act of gifting." *(Sunan Abu-Dawud)*

By action Nabi ﷺ had made it clear that true sympathy is not that one agrees to everything said or done by ones fellowmen or companions, but true sympathy is to be able to rectify the wrongs of ones fellowmen and friends by correcting them and guiding them away from evil habits and mannerisms.

Who should I show most kindness too?

A man cam into the court of Nabi ﷺ and asked, "Who is most deserving of my kindness?" Nabi ﷺ said, "Your mother!" The man asked, "Thereafter who deserves my kindness?" Nabi ﷺ said, "Your mother!" He again asked, "Thereafter who deserves my kindness?" For the third time Nabi ﷺ said, "Your mother!" When asked for the forth time, Thereafter who deserves my kindness?" Nabi ﷺ said, "Your father!" *(Bukhari)*

The blessing of showing kindness to ones parents:

On one occasion Nabi ﷺ explained the blessings one can achieve by serving ones parents by means of an amazing incident:

Amongst the people gone by, there were three people travelling when suddenly they were afflicted by a heavy down pour of rain. They ran towards a cave in a nearby mountain to seek refuge from the rain. Whilst inside the cave, a boulder rolled over and covered the mouth of the cave causing them to be trapped within. They first experienced one difficulty in the form of rain, now they had an added woe.

Now to get out of this situation they had no avenue but to turn to Allaah and ask him for salvation. It was decided that each one will supplicate to Allaah presenting one such action done in his life solely for the pleasure of Allaah. So this is what they did.

The first person supplicated thus: "O Allaah you are well aware that I had aged parents and young children. Everyday I would take our goats out to graze as this was our means of sustenance. It was my habit that when I would return in the evening, after having milked the goats I would first present the milk to my parents. Only after they would drink I would give my children to drink.

One day I went out a distance to graze the goats and therefore returned home very late. By this time my parents had already fallen asleep. As was my daily habit, I milked the goats and brought the milk to my parents but found them fast asleep. I felt it inappropriate to wake them up and neither did I like to give anyone to drink of the milk before them. I therefore stood at their head side intending to give them the milk as soon as they awoke. On the other hand the children were crying at my feet out of hunger, but I refused to give them any milk before my parents. In this way the entire night passed until daybreak.

O Allaah you know very well that this act (of showing kindness to my parents) was done solely for your pleasure, therefore remove us from this difficulty."

His supplication was accepted to the extent that the boulder moved enough for them to be able to see the skyline and breathe more easily. In similar manner the other two also supplicated presenting their deeds until they were granted salvation and freed from the cave. (The supplication of the first was in connection with parents therefore it was mentioned here. The supplication of the other two could be found in Bukhari Shareef under the chapter Kitaabul Aadaab and in Muslim Shareef under the chapter Kitaabuzhikri wad-duaai wat-toubah)

Dear children, this is the colour service towards parents bring about. It becomes a means of salvation in this world and in the hereafter. It is also a means of earning the pleasure of Allaah and great rewards in the hereafter. Therefore we should all make it binding upon ourselves we will serve our parents in accordance with the commands of Allaah and the practice of Nabi ﷺ so that Allaah becomes pleased with us and we can attain success in this world and the hereafter. We ask Allaah to give us the ability to practice. Aameen

Chapter 3:

Teaching children with love and affection:

A child is advised not to throw stones at dates:

Hadhrat Amar Ibn Absa ﷺ narrates the following incident of his in these words:

As young boy I would go into the date gardens of the Ansaar and break dates of the trees by throwing stones at them. **One day they caught me and brought me to Nabi﷽ complaining about my action. Nabi ﷺ asked me why** I threw stones at the dates and I said so that I could drop them from the tree.

Nabi ﷺ then advised me thus, "**Do not** throw stones at the dates, **but eat** that which **falls** off the trees." (He advised him thus as throwing stones harms the trees.) He **then placed his hand over my head and made the following dua**, "O Allaah you satiate his stomach." *(Abu-Dawud)*

In other words, with great love and affection he thought him that he should not throw stones at the trees, but eat that which fell off the trees, and in the same breath he made dua for him.

Nabi ﷺ teaches a child how to skin an animal:

Hadhrat Abu Saeed Khudri ﷜ narrates that Nabi ﷺ passed by a child of approximately twelve to thirteen years of age whilst the child was busy skinning an animal.

He told the lad, "Hang on. **Let me show you** how to skin an animal."

He then placed his fist between the skin and body of the animal pushing his hand forward until he reached the shoulder of the animal. He then told the lad, "Now this is how you skin an animal."

Nabi ﷺ then went to the Masjid and lead the congregation in salah without renewing his ablution (*wudhu*). *(Ibn-Majah)*

Let me teach you a few lessons, son:

Hadhrat Ibn Abbaas ﷜ says that he was once travelling on the same conveyance as Nabi ﷺ was seated behind. Nabi ﷺ addressed him thus, "I would like to teach you a few lessons. Protect the commands of Allaah and he will protect you. Implement the orders of Allaah and you will always find Him before you. When you ask, ask of Allaah alone. When you seek assistance, seek assistance from Allaah alone. Remember, if the entire creation has to gather and try to bring benefit to you in any way, they will not be able to benefit you accept to the extent decreed for you. Remember, if the entire creation has to try and cause harm to you, they will not be able to cause any harm to accept to the extent decreed for you." *(Musnad-e-Ahmed)*

Rasulullaah ﷺ first turned his attention towards himself, and then taught him the above mentioned important lessons. Those parents to whom this Hadith reaches via this Kitaab are urged to affectionately teach their children these important lessons of life. This is binding upon you as a parent. Children are also urged to extract time from their parents for purposes of learning such lessons as this is your right.

Do not make a live object your target, children:

Nabi ﷺ once saw a few children from amongst the Ansaar playing at a certain spot. **Since Nabi ﷺ had encouraged archery, these children had tied a chicken and made it their target.** Nabi ﷺ immediately stopped them and told them not to cause pain to something with life in this manner. *(Musnad-e-Ahmed)*

Nabi ﷺ himself used to practice archery and so did the Sahaba ﷺ practice archery. That is why in the above mentioned incident we find that he did not discourage them from archery, but he prohibited them from making a live object the target when practicing. **Leave alone Human Beings, Islaam prohibits one from causing harm to animals even!**

On one occasion Nabi ﷺ noticed that a person had set alight an ant hill. He immediately prohibited him from this and told him that only Allaah has the right to inflict punishment by means of fire.

Take the name and partake of the meals dear son:

There used to be a young Sahabi by the name of Umar Ibn Abi Salamah ﷺ in the spiritual care of Nabi ﷺ.

He was one day sitting and partaking of meals with Nabi ﷺ. He himself narrates that he had been eating in a manner whereby he was taking food from all ends of the utensil. Nabi ﷺ noticed this and addressed him saying, **"Dear son, take the name of Allaah before eating, eat using the right hand and eat from that which is directly in front of you."** He says that ever since this occasion he always practiced on the teaching of Nabi ﷺ. *(Bukhari)*

Do you not see with what love and affection our master Nabi ﷺ trained and nurtured the children? In this way he taught them the Islaamic etiquettes of life.

Nabi ﷺ removes a date from the mouth of his grandson:

Hadhrat Abu Hurairah ﷜ narrates that on one occasion when the time of harvesting the dates had approached, and the Sahaba ﷞ began to bring the agricultural tax due on them and that which they had intended giving away in charity to Nabi ﷺ, a large heap of dates had collected. Hadhrat Hasan ﷜ and Hadhrat Husain ﷜ were little children at that time and had been playing nearby the heap of dates. One of them picked up a date and put it into his mouth. Suddenly Nabi ﷺ gaze fell on him. He immediately went up to him, placed his finger in his mouth and removed the date saying, "Dear son, remember that we cannot accept charity." *(In other words it is not permissible for the family of Nabi ﷺ to accept charity.)*

Under the same chapter in another narration it is mentioned that Nabi ﷺ used the words *'kakh kakh'* (Spit it out! Spit it out!) to remove the date from the child's mouth. *(Bukhari)*

In the narration of Musnad-e-Ahmed the child who picked up the date is said to be Hadhrat Hasan ﷜.

By way of example Nabi ﷺ has illustrated to us that children should be taught with love and affection, but when it comes to the commands of Allaah, and then no one but Allaah is taken into consideration. Those dates were meant for the poor Muslims therefore Nabi ﷺ did not allow his grandson to eat a single date from it as it should only reach those who have a right in it.

Why is the hair of this boy long on some parts of the head and short on other parts?

Nabi ﷺ once noticed that a youngster's hair was cut in such a manner that some of his hair was long and the rest was short. He reprimanded him by saying that this should not be done. **Either the hair is left to grow all at one length or it is cut equally all around.** *(Nasai)*

There was time when Muslims were influenced by a Hindu custom where a pony tail was grown. Nowadays the Western culture has modified this culture by cutting the hair in a manner that some parts are long and other parts are short. Definitely this culture is as shallow and despicable as the Hindu culture! Why should we therefore turn to these cultures and when we have a pure and pristine culture of our own?

All praises are due to Allaah who has saved this child from the fire of Jahannam:

There used to be a youngster who used to come in the gatherings of Nabi ﷺ although he was not a Muslim. He was in fact a Jewish youngster but he had great love and confidence in Nabi ﷺ and for this reason he would even serve Nabi ﷺ.

A few days passed by and this youngster did not come to the gatherings of Nabi ﷺ. It was later learnt that he has taken ill. Nabi ﷺ accompanied by a few companions went to visit this youngster. When Nabi ﷺ realised that he was on his death bed, he immediately invited him to Islaam. The boy turned to his father who was at his head side for permission and approval. **The father said, "Obey Abul Qasim!"** *(Nabi ﷺ title was Abul Qasim.)*

After being given permission by his father the youngster accepted Islaam. He testified that there was none worthy of worship in truth except Allaah and Muhammed ﷺ was His servant and Rasul-messenger. This brought great joy to the heart of Nabi ﷺ who praised Allaah saying, "All praises are due to Allaah who has saved his soul from Jahannam by means of me!" *(Bukhari)*

In the narration of Musnad-e-Ahmed it is mentioned that Nabi ﷺ had told the Sahaba ﺭﺿﻲ ﺍﻟﻠﻪ ﺗﻌﺎﻟﻰ to ensure that they performed janazah salah over the youngster. He was then buried in the Muslim cemetery. It has been reported in the commentary of Bukhari Shareef, Fathul Bari, that the boy's name was Abdul-Quddoos. Allaah knows best.

We learn from reading the above incident that our noble master even visited children when they were sick. He also always encouraged them towards good. Above all he gave them the opportunity to serve him.

It is therefore imperative that we learn the teachings of our noble master, understand them and inform our other brothers and sisters with regards to them so that we can all practically implement them in our lives.

Virtues of sending
salutations upon Nabi ﷺ

Remember well dear children, if we wish to be successful we will have to follow Nabi ﷺ and show great love for him. From amongst the etiquettes of expressing our love for him we learn that whenever we hear or read his name we should send salutations upon him. It is the saying of Nabi ﷺ that he who hears his name and does not send salutations upon him is indeed a miser. *(Thirmizi)*

Now let us vow to send salutations upon Nabi ﷺ every time we come across or hear his name. You should be knowing which form of durood (salutation) is best? Remember that form of durood is most virtuous which was taught to the Sahaba رضى الله تعالى عنه by Nabi ﷺ himself.

A group of Sahaba رضى الله تعالى عنه once came to Nabi ﷺ and said, "We have learnt how to send greetings to you by means of the dua read in tashahhud, but who should send our salutations upon you?" Nabi ﷺ said, "You should do so in the following words, *'Allaahuma salli alaa Muhammadiw wa alaa aali Muhammadin kama sallaita alaa Ebrahima wa alaa aali Ebrahima innaka hameedum majeed. Allaahuma baarik alaa Muhammadiw wa alaa aali Muhammadin kama baarakta alaa Ebrahima wa alaa aali Ebrahima innaka hameedum majeed.'"* (Bukhari Shareef)

We learn that this form of durood was taught by Nabi ﷺ himself and was beloved to him. We ask Allaah to give us the ability to send durood in abundance to Nabi ﷺ. Aameen.

It has been reported that Nabi ﷺ has said, "He who sends the most durood upon me will be closest to me on the Day of Judgement." *(Thirmizi)*

Let us look at another beautiful Hadith narrated by Hadhrat Abu Hurairah رضي الله تعالى عنه wherein Nabi ﷺ is reported to have said, "He who writes down salutations upon me on any piece of paper, the angels continue seeking forgiveness on behalf of him so long as that paper remains." *(Tabrani)*

Incidents narrated by Nabi ﷺ to the Sahaba رضي الله تعالى عنه relating to nations of the past:

Our noble master had narrated certain incidents related to the nations of the past which are found in the books of Ahaadith. Perhaps you may want to read a few of them.

A real mother's love for her child:

Hadhrat Abu Hurairah رضي الله تعالى عنه narrates from Nabi ﷺ that there were two women in a nation gone by. One was elderly and the other was young. The two of them were going along, each one with a child when a wolf suddenly snatched one of the children. A dispute now ensued. The elder one claimed that the wolf had snatched the younger ones child, while the younger claimed that the wolf snatched the older ones child. They finally agreed to bring the matter to Hadhrat Dawud عليه الصلاة والسلام so that he could make a decision.

After hearing the case, the decision was made in favour of the older woman. As they left, they met up with **Suleiman** عليه الصلاة والسلام along the way. He was the son of Dawud رضي الله تعالى عنه who was also a Nabi. He asked them as to what decision was made. The younger one spoke up and immediately said that the decision was made in favour of the older woman. (Sensing what had happened) he asked for a knife and **said that he was going to cut the child in two and give each one half the child. The younger of the two spontaneously spoke up that he should rather just give the child to the older woman.** Suleiman عليه السلام thus figured that the child has got to be the younger ones and therefore amended the decision in favour of the younger woman and made over the child to her. *(Bukhari Shareef)*

Three children who spoke from the cradle:

Hadhrat Abu Hurairah رضي الله تعالى عنه narrates from Nabi ﷺ that there were three children from the nations of the past who spoke from the cradle. (In other words they spoke before the normal age at which a child begins to speak.)

1. **Eesa** عليه السلام **is one of them** and his incident is mentioned in the Quraan itself under chapter 16 in Surah Mariam. The crux of the incident is as follows. Hadhrat Mariam عليها السلام was unmarried when Jibraeel عليه السلام was ordered by Allaah to blow into her sleeve by means of which Allaah caused her to conceive. When Eesa عليه السلام was born and she came to her people carrying him, her nation began to rebuke her saying that she hails from a chaste family. How could she beget a child whereas she is unmarried?

People now began thinking ill of her. At this precise time Allaah gave Eesa عليه السلام the ability to speak whilst still in the cradle! He said, "Verily I am the servant of Allaah. He has given me a (divine) book and made me a Nabi-prophet." *(Surah Mariam)*

This was the incident of Eesa عليه السلام speaking during his infancy and giving testimony to the chastity of his mother.

2. **The worshipper from Bani Israaeel named Juraij.**
    The second child who spoke before the normal age at
    which a child begins to speak, was a child who gave
    testimony in favour of a worshipper from amongst the
    Bani Israaeel named Juraij. The details of his incident
    are as follows.

Juraij was an ardent worshipper of Allaah from
amongst the Bani Israaeel who had built himself a place of
worship wherein he would worship Allaah. One day whilst
engaged in salah his mother came to him and called out to
him to do some work for her. Due to him being engaged in
salah, he began to ask himself in his heart, "O Allaah my
mother or my salah?" He then chose to continue with his
salah.

The next day while engaged in salah again, his mother
came to him and called out to him to do some work for her.
He again began to ask himself, "O Allaah my mother or my
salah?" For the second time he chose to continue with his
salah.

On the third day again whilst he was busy with his salah his
mother came out to him and called out to him to do some
work for her. Again he chose to continue with his salah.
**His mother blurted out a curse on him saying, "You
should not die until you see the face of an unchaste
woman!"**

Now the level of worship found in Juraij became
common talk amongst his people. One day a woman who
was known for her beauty said to the people, "If you people
say so, I will seduce Juraij!" The people began to wonder
how she would be able to do such a thing.

Nevertheless, she beautified herself and came to the
worship place of Juraij and tried to seduce him, but he was

unmoved and least intimidated. She now decided to come up with an evil scheme. There used to be a shepherd in the area who used to spend the night in the worship place of Juraij. She seduced this shepherd and fell pregnant as a result of the affair. When the child was born, she began claiming that the child was as a result of an illicit relationship with Juraij!

The people began to rebuke Juraij and beat him up. They even razed his place of worship to the ground. He asked them what was all this about. They said that he had committed adultery with such and such woman and she has now given birth to his child. Juraij asked them where was the child and that they should bring the child to him. In the meantime he engaged himself in salah. **When the child was brought to him he addressed the child and asked the child who his father really was. This child who was but just a few days old spoke out, "My father is so and so shepherd!"**

The people now became astonished that a new born child is even giving testimony to his chastity. They were now convinced as regards his piety and began to trust him and believed him to be a true person. They asked him for forgiveness and even offered to rebuild his place of worship from gold. He refused the offer and asked them to rebuild it in its original clay form.

The third child who spoke before the normal age of speaking:

A woman from amongst the Bani Israaeel was busy breast feeding her child when a person passed by. This person was well dressed, moved with elegance and rode a strong conveyance. The mother said, "O Allaah make my child like this person." The child left the breast of the mother and looked towards the person saying, "O Allaah do not make me like him!" (In reality this person was an oppressive and haughty person full of pride.)

The child then resumed suckling on his mother. The Sahabi who narrates this incident says that Nabi ﷺ even took his index finger and sucked on it showing how the child was suckling on his mother.

A short while later a group of people passed by this mother and child. These people were hitting a woman and saying to her, "You have committed adultery and you are also a thief." All the woman said was, "Allaah is sufficient for me and he is the best of ambassadors." The mother said, "O Allaah do not make my child like her." The child turned away from the breast of the mother looking towards the woman and said, "O Allaah make me like her!" (In reality this woman was an obedient slave of Allaah and the people were unjustifiably beating her. Through the will and permission of Allaah this little child made dua to Allaah to make him from amongst his obedient servants.)

These were the incidents of three children narrated by Nabi ﷺ to the Sahaba رضوان الله تعالى عنهم. They had spoken before the normal age of speech. *(Muslim Shareef)*

Thousands accept Islaam on the steadfastness of the Imaan of one young child:

Nabi ﷺ once narrated the following incident to the Sahaba رضوان الله تعالى عنهم.

Amongst a nation of the past lived a king who had an experienced sorcerer who used to do the act of sorcery in the kingdom. When he became old and was approaching his death, he asked the king to find a young intelligent boy in the kingdom whom he could teach his sorcery to so that when he dies the boy can continue with his sorcery as it seems that his death was imminent.

Therefore a young intelligent boy was found who was to learn the sorcery from him. On the way to the sorcerer the boy had to pass by a monk who used to be engaged in the worship of Allaah and dissemination of knowledge. The boy would stand and listen to his sermons and thus turn up late at the sorcerer. On his return he would stop again and thus return home late. The sorcerer used to reprimand him and beat him for being late, while his parents would also reprimand him and beat him for being late. One day the boy complained to the monk that this is what happened everyday. **The monk told him that he should tell the sorcerer that his family had delayed him, and he should tell his family that the sorcerer delayed him.** Times passed by in this way that he would on one hand learn sorcery and on the other hand learn the Deen of Allaah.

One day on his way he noticed that the road ahead was blocked by a vicious animal and therefore people could not go pass. He began to think in his heart that today was the perfect day to test whether the monk or sorcerer was on the truth. He then picked up a stone and saying, "O Allaah if you regard the monks teaching as the truth and the sorcerer's sorcery as falsehood, then destroy this animal and clear these peoples path." He then threw the stone at the animal instantly killing it. The road was thus opened and the boy now became popular.

He then told the monk what had transpired. The monk told him, "Son, you have surpassed me; you will now be tested by Allaah. Do not tell anyone about me." People now began to flock at the boys' feet with their needs requesting him to make dua for them. In this way many an ill person was cured through the blessings of his dua. **There was a minister in the ministry of the king who was blind.** Hearing about the youngster he came to him with many gifts seeking dua from him to be cured. He told the boy, "If you cure me, I will give you all these gifts." The boy said, **"Cure is not in my hands. Cure is in the hands of Allaah who is my Rabb and your Rabb.** If you promise to bring Imaan in him I will make dua to him that he cures you." The minister agreed to this and the boy made dua for him. Allaah cured the minister and he brought Imaan on Allaah as he had promised.

The minister returned to the court of the king and began doing the tasks he used to do prior to him becoming blind. The king was quite surprised and asked him as to who had restored his eyesight. The minister said, "My Allaah has restored my eyesight." (The king considered himself to be the Rabb of his subjects) therefore he became enraged and asked him, "Do you have a Rabb other than me?" The minister said, **"My Rabb and your Rabb is Allaah."** The king disliked such talk and beat the minister asking him where he had learnt this. He informed the king about the boy. The king summoned the boy and questioned him thus, "You have leant sorcery and you now cure the sick by means of your sorcery?" The boy answered him thus, **"Neither I nor the sorcery of anyone can cure the sick. Cure is solely in the hands of my Allaah."** The king asked, "You mean; in my hands?" The boy said, "Certainly not! Your Rabb and my Rabb is none other than Allaah." The king now enraged said, "In other words you are implying that there is a Rabb other than myself?" The boy, unaffected said, **"My Rabb, your Rabb and the Rabb of everyone is Allaah who is alone and has no partner."** This made the king very, very angry.

All types of punishment were now inflicted on the boy so that he may denounce his belief and believe in the king as his Rabb. With continuous punishment he was even forced to disclose the whereabouts of the monk. The monk was summoned into the court of the king and told to denounce his belief which he refused to do so. The king ordered that he be sawed in two and his body should be disposed off. The minister was then summoned and told to denounce his belief. He refused to do so and was therefore also killed.

He now called the boy and told him that he still had a chance to denounce his belief and believe in the king as his Rabb. The boy was firm and steadfast and refused to accept the proposal of the king. The king then called a few soldiers and ordered them to take the boy to the top of a mountain and once again tell him to forsake his religion. Should he still refuse, they should throw him of the mountain. So they took him up the mountain and decided to throw him off. He supplicated to Allaah thus, **"O Allaah you suffice for me however you so wish."** No sooner did he make the dua, than the mountain began to tremble and the soldiers all plunged to there death, and the boy was saved.

The boy returned to the court of the king. The king asked, "Where have the soldiers gone?" The boy told him that his Allaah had saved him from them and destroyed them. The king called some other soldiers and ordered them to take him on a ship into the middle of the ocean and throw him into the sea! When these soldiers took him to the middle of the ocean and intended throwing him in, he supplicated to Allaah in the like manner saying, **"O Allaah you suffice for me however you so wish."** Immediately on his dua a wave rose and drowned all the soldiers sparing the boy. He once again returned to the court of the king and told him that his Allaah had saved him yet again from the soldiers. He also told the king that he may adopt any means to try and kill him, but he will fail. Yes, if he wanted to kill

him there was one way by means of which he would
definitely kill him, and that is he should gather all the
people in one massive open field. Here he should build a
gallows from date trees and then take him (the boy) to the
gallows. **Thereafter he should take an arrow from the
youths quiver, place it on a bow and say, 'In the name
of the Rabb of this boy' then shoot the arrow. If Allaah
wills then this method will kill him.**

So the king did as he was told. The arrow struck the
youth on his temple, he lifted his hand and placed it on is
temple and became a martyr! His martyrdom made the
people who had gathered there realise that his religion was
indeed the true religion and this made them bring
conviction in Allaah. **From all four sides the cry of 'We
believe in the Rabb of this youth, we believe in the Rabb
of this youth' could now be heard.** The people now no
longer believed in the king as their Rabb. Witnessing this,
the king and his courtiers now became very worried. They
began to say that they had actually not understood the plan
of the youth. Now that has happened which they had all
along feared. All these people have come onto the
youths'Deen whereas the youth was put to the gallows for
the very reason that it would put a stop to his Deen! Now
what should they do? The king ordered that trenches be dug
all over, sticks should be thrown into these trenches and
ignited so that no person can escape...............those who
believe in the Rabb of the youth should be thrown in to
these trenches.

The people preferred being thrown into the burning
trenches, but were in no way prepared to forsake their true
belief. **Amongst them was a woman who had a suckling
baby and due to her love for this baby was hesitant to
jump into the trench. (Allaah gave this suckling baby
the ability to talk and say,) "O my mother, be patient**

and jump into the fire!" (Muslim Shareef) The people of
Imaan were all killed in this way and the youth was also
buried with them in the trench.

An amazing fact is mentioned after this Hadith in
Thirmizi Shareef and that is as follows.
During the Khilafat of Umar ﷺ that particular spot
was dug up and the corpse of the youth was found intact
with his hand still on his temple as it was at the time of his
martyrdom! *(Thirmizi – under the commentary of Surah
Burooj)*

The journey of a young child
from the darkness of Kufr
to the light of Islaam:

**This is the incident of child by the name of Maa-
bihi.** It is quite lengthy, though very interesting and we
could learn many lessons from it.

There used to be a wealthy family known as 'Aabul
mulk' in a town called **'Jee'** which was situated **in Persia
(modern day Iran).** Their leaders' name was Borzakhshan
Bin Morsalaan Aabul mulki. He was a prominent and
influential person in the court of the Persian king. He was
not just wealthy, but a very staunch fire worshipper. He had
an only son by the name of Maa-bihi whom he most dearly
loved. He brought him up with great pomp and show. In
spite of the parents' great aspirations, he was to be an
honoured person. He was never a proud person nor was he
a mischievous child. Instead of spending his time playing
with the other kids of his age, he would spend his time
ensuring that the fire which was worshipped never burnt
out.

One day Borzakhshan told his son Maa-bihi that he had some important work and therefore he could not attend to his farm lands, so Maa-bihi should do a check on the lands for him. In fulfilment of his fathers' command he immediately set out for the fields. On his way he passed by a church wherein the congregation was busy praying in a loud voice. Hearing their voices he entered the church and was greatly affected by their method of prayer and immediately shunned his belief of fire worship. When the Christians had completed their prayer, he told the priest that he liked the way they prayed and from that day on he wished to discard fire worship and enter into Christianity. The priest became elated and immediately baptised him and brought him into the fold of Christianity.

The desire for the true religion (of that time,) Christianity became deeply embedded in the heart of Maa-bihi. He asked them where was there central church. **They told him that it was in Syria.** Nevertheless, he remained at the church for the rest of the day. When the sun had set he returned home. His father asked him if he had checked on the fields. He said that he had not done so as he had seen a church on his way and was affected by the way the people in the church were praying and he therefore remained there all day long. The father became very angry and told him that their religion was no good and that he was now grounded and will not be able to leave the house anymore. He also put shackles on his feet so that he could not go anywhere. He somehow found an opportunity to send a message to the people of the church that they should inform him of any caravan going towards Syria.

He was informed one day that a caravan was going. He managed to free himself from the shackles and joined the caravan. **Upon reaching Syria** he enquired about the pope and immediately went to the pope to serve him. He told the pope that he had left Persia and come to him to learn the

religion of Christianity. The pope agreed to keep him in his
company. Now this particular pope was outwardly a very
pious and abstinent person, but on the inside he was greedy
for wealth and he used to rob the people of their wealth in
devious ways. Maa-bihi did not like the ways and habits of
the pope but could not do much. After some time the pope
died. When the people gathered to prepare for the burial of
the pope, Maa-bihi revealed his secret. The people were
enraged and instead, they took him and hung him on the
gallows! His successor was however a pious person who
had no inclination for the things of this world. Maa-bihi
had firm faith in him and served him, heart and soul. The
pope also made every effort to pass on his bounty to him.
As the life of this pope now neared its end, he told Maa-
bihi that he should **go to a certain person in a place called
'Mousil'** as he would not find any one other than that
person on the true religion.

Now Maa-bihi finally reached Mousil as the pope had
bequeathed after much difficulty. Here he began to serve
this person and acquire knowledge from him. Allaah had
planned that not too long after this person also embarked on
his journey to the hereafter. At the time of his death he told
Maa-bihi: **Dear son, after you have buried me you
should go to a person at a place called 'Naseebeen'.** In
my opinion he is the only person on the true religion. The
rest of the people have changed the religion deviated from
the straight path.

In search of the truth Maa-bihi now reached Naseebeen
and began to serve the priest of this area. He had hardly
gained from his bounty when death made him a morsel
also. A short while before his death Maa-bihi had asked
him for advice **He was told the truth which he was in
search of coul l be found by a person in a place called
'Umoodiah'.**

So Maa-bihi turned his steps towards Umoodiah where he began to serve the bishop there. This particular bishop was bestowed with knowledge and practice. He was true follower of the deen of Eesa ﷺ. Maa-bihi benefited a great deal from his bounty and now also began to engage in different forms of worship with a great deal of enthusiasm. During his free time, for the benefit of his personal needs, Maa-bihi had purchased and reared a few cattle and goats. Life went on until the time came for this pious person of Umoodiah to leave this world.

Maa-bihi asked him, "I have travelled thousands of miles with great difficulty and knocked at the door of many before I reached you. Now you are also leaving this world. Where should I go from here?"

This pious man of Umoodiah now in the throws of death addressed him thus, "O the one who seeks the truth. What should I tell you? At this time and era everyone seems to be drowning in the ocean of sin. The lightening of Kufr and Shirk is striking everywhere. I do not know of anyone to whom I can send you. **Yes, if there is any place I can guide you towards, is a land in the desserts of Arabia where the final Nabi-prophet will rise and bring alive the true religion. He will migrate to a land where dates could be found in abundance. He will have the seal of Nabuwaat-prophethood between his shoulder blades; he will accept gifts but not charity.** If you live until his time, then you ensure that you serve him."

Giving these last words of advice, this bishop also left the world and headed towards the hereafter. Here was Maa-bihi in search of the beautiful light of the last Nabi. He had now become impatient and was constantly awaiting a caravan going in the direction of his quest. His wish finally came true. He learnt that a caravan of Banu Kalb was going to pass by that way on their way to the blessed lands. He immediately went to the leader of the caravan and told him that he had some livestock which he was prepared to exchange in return for them taking him along with them to the blessed lands. He instantly agreed and took possession of the livestock and allowed Maa-bihi to join the caravan. **The caravan finally reached Makkah.** The intentions of the travellers of this particular caravan changed as regards this innocent youngster. They enslaved him and sold him to a Jew of Makkah. He remained with the Jew for some time as a slave. One day, a relative of this Jew from Madeenah had come to visit him and he also required a slave. He mentioned this to his host who sold Maa-bihi to him. **Maa-bihi now travelled along with this person to Madeenah whereupon reaching he had found it to be place of date trees in abundance.** He was elated and realised that he had almost reached his quest and this has got to be the place with regards to which the bishop of Umoodiah had made mention off. Now he spent everyday and every night restlessly waiting to find that final Nabi.

That joyous day finally arrived which Maa-bihi had so long awaited. He had climbed a date tree of his Jewish master and was busy breaking dates while the Jew was sitting at the bottom. Suddenly another Jew came running from the direction of the city calling out to his master. Upon reaching Maa-bihi and his master, the Jew began saying, "Almighty must destroy Banu Qailah! They are all flocking to a man at Quba who has come from Makkah and claims to be the final Nabi. They have accepted his invitation, men, woman and children!"

These words reached the ears of Maa-bihi and brought joy to his entire body. His heart testified that this was certainly the object of his quest. He involuntarily climbed off the tree and asked the Jew who had come with the news to repeat himself. His master became angry at him for taking interest in this news and rebuked him. He told him

that it was none of his business and he should get along
with his work.

Now dear children, I am sure you are well aware who
this person in Quba was? Yes, he was certainly your Nabi
and my Nabi, the last and final of all Nabi's.

Now Maa-bihi awaited the opportunity until it arrived.
He went into the market and purchased a few items which
he brought to Nabi ﷺ. He presented it to him saying, "O
the chosen servant of Allaah, you and your companions are
outsiders, I have therefore brought these few items as
charity for all of you as I find no one more deserving of it
than you. Please accept it from me."

Nabi ﷺ accepted these items from Maa-bihi and
made them over to his companions telling them that they
should partake of it. He cannot partake of it as they are
items of charity. Maa-bihi had found proof of the first sign.
The next day he bought a few items which he brought to
Nabi ﷺ and presented it to him saying, "Please accept
this gift from me." Nabi ﷺ willingly accepted the gift and
he ate from it and also gave his companions to eat from it.
The second sign was now proven, the sign of him accepting
gifts. All that was left was to see the third and final sign.
That was the seal of Nabuwaat-prophethood.

A few days later Maa-bihi learnt that Nabi ﷺ was
going to attend a certain janazah. He hurriedly reached
Nabi ﷺ and most respectfully greeted him. Now he
impatiently awaited the opportunity to witness the seal of
Nabuwaat-prophethood on the back of Rasulullaah ﷺ.
Nabi ﷺ perceived what was going through the heart of
Maa-bihi, so he moved the clothing on his back enough for
him to witness the seal. Here was the seal of Nabuwaat-
prophethood glaring at Maa-bihi in the face! Out of
reverence and respect he bowed down and with shivering

lips kissed the seal of Nabuwaat-prophethood! He then began crying involuntarily. Nabi ﷺ asked him to come to the front, which he obligingly did. He then narrated all the stages he had gone through to get to Nabi ﷺ and the truth from beginning to end.

Nabi ﷺ then narrated the entire story of Maa-bihi to his Sahaba رضى الله تعالى عنه. Maa-bihi then accepted Islaam at the hands of Nabi ﷺ who gave him a Muslim name. Maa-bihi Bin Borzakhshan was from then on known as the great and prominent Sahabi by the name of Salmaan Farsi رضى الله تعالى عنه.

A revolution had now taken place in the life of Salmaan Farsi رضى الله تعالى عنه who desired to be in the companionship of Nabi ﷺ day and night but was unable to do so as he was bound by the yoke of slavery at the hands of the Jew. As a result he was deprived of participating in the battles of Badr and Uhud.

Nabi ﷺ was aware of the difficulty of Salmaan Farsi رضى الله تعالى عنه. One day he told him, "O Salmaan! Why do you not barter your freedom from your master and free yourself from slavery."

This was exactly what Salmaan رضى الله تعالى عنه had desired, so he went to his master and asked him what was the price for his freedom. **The Jew asked for 40 uqiyah of gold and 300 date palms!** Upon hearing the Jews' demands, Nabi ﷺ asked his companions as to who was willing to free Salmaan رضى الله تعالى عنه from the slavery of the oppressive Jew. The Sahaba رضى الله تعالى عنه responded with great joy at the request of Nabi ﷺ each one bringing whatever he could until they had collected 300 date palms. Then all of them together with Nabi ﷺ began ploughing the land and sowing the seeds of these palms on the land of the Jew. Now the condition of the 40 uqiyah only remained. Allaah made arrangements for this to be fulfilled in a short time. Not long after the required amount came into the possession of the Muslims in the form of booty from a battle which the Muslims had fought. Nabi ﷺ made over the amount to Salmaan رضي الله تعالى عنه and told him to go and free himself. Salmaan رضي الله تعالى عنه ran to the Jew with the amount and freed himself throwing the yoke of slavery of his head. From now on he perpetually remained in the service of Nabi ﷺ.

Chapter 5:

Sayings of Nabi ﷺ and incidents relating to parent's rights over children:

We are commanded in the Quraan to show kindness towards our parents and we also find many ahaadith relating to this subject. The hadith is famous wherein Nabiﷺ is reported to have said, "Jannat lays beneath the feet of the mother." *(Mishkat; with reference from Ahmed and Nasai)*

Nabi ﷺ is reported to have said that the pleasure of Allaah is in pleasing ones father and the displeasure of Allaah is in displeasing ones father. *(Ibn-Majah)*

On one occasion Nabi ﷺ mentioned four major sins. The first on the list was; disobedience towards the mother. He also said, "Allaah has made disobedience of the mother forbidden upon you." *(Bukhari)*

Nabi ﷺ was once seated in a gathering. All those around him were sitting attentively. He said, "He is indeed a wretched person! He is indeed a wretched person! He is indeed a wretched person!" His companions asked him, "Who O Rasul-messenger of Allaah تَبَارَكَوَتَعَالَ?" Nabi ﷺ said, "That person whose parents (both parents) or either one of them (parents) attain old age and he/she (the child) fails to earn jannat by serving them!" *(Muslim Shareef)*

Whilst in another gathering a person asked Nabi ﷺ, "Which action of ours is most beloved in the sight of Allaah?" Nabi ﷺ, "Observing Salah on its prescribed time." The person asked, "Thereafter which action?" Nabi ﷺ said, "Showing kindness towards ones parents." The person asked, "Thereafter which action?" Nabi ﷺ said, "Striving in the path of Allaah." *(Bukhari)*

A person came to Nabi ﷺ and informed him that he committed a sin and wanted to know if there was any way he could be forgiven. Nabi ﷺ asked him if his mother was alive. He replied in the negative. Nabi ﷺ then asked him if his mothers' sister was alive. He said that she was alive. Nabi ﷺ then advised him to be very kind towards his aunt. In other words this would serve as atonement for his sin! *(Thirmizi)*

Parents should never be sworn at:

The leader of all the Muhadditheen, Imam Muhammed Ibn Ismail Bukhari has narrated the following hadith in his compilation:

From amongst the major sins is the sin of swearing at ones' parents. A Sahabi ﵁ asked if it were possible that one would swear his/her parents? Nabi ﷺ said; a person swears the parents of another, he in turn swears the parents of the person who swore his/her parents. Nabi ﷺ implied that the person, who first swore at the other persons' parents, has in reality sworn his own parents due to the second person reciprocating the swearing. (Bukhari)

Join ties with ones mother even though she is disobedient

Hadhrat Asmaa Bint Abu Bakr ﵂ once asked Nabi ﷺ if she should maintain ties with her mother who visits her but has not yet embraced Islaam? Nabi ﷺ advised her that she should keep ties with her. In other words she should not sever ties from them, but show absolute kindness towards them.

This shows that, irrespective of whether the mother is fortunate and has correct beliefs or unfortunate and has incorrect beliefs, she is still the mother and therefore deserving of her children's respect. *(Bukhari)*

Parents' stages are raised in the hereafter as a result of his/her child seeking forgiveness on his/her behalf:

Nabi ﷺ is reported to have said that a persons' stages will be elevated in the hereafter as a result of his/her child seeking forgiveness on his/her behalf. He/she will ask, "Why are my stages being elevated?" It will be told, "As a result of your child seeking forgiveness for you!" *(Ibn-Majah)*

Dear children, May Allaah keep your parents at ease and allow them to give you the best upbringing. You should continue serving your parents during their lifetime and seek forgiveness on behalf of them after their demise so that Allaah forgives them and elevates their stages.

They are your heaven (jannat) or hell (jahannam):

Hadhrat Abu Umaamah ﷺ narrates that a person came to Nabi ﷺ and asked him as to what were the rights of parents over their children. Nabi ﷺ replied that they are either your jannat or jahannam. *(Ibn-Majah)*

This implies that a person who will obey his parents will thereby earn his jannat and that person who disobeys his parents will not only suffer the consequences in the life of this world, but will as a result suffer in the hereafter as well. We make dua that Allaah gives every child the ability to obey his/her parents and protect every child from being disobedient to his/her parents.

There is yet another hadith which emphasizes the importance of revering the father. The details of which, are somewhat as follows.

Rasulullaah ﷺ once told a Sahabi رضي الله تعالى عنه that the father is a middle door from the doors of jannat. One may maintain this door (by being obedient to ones father) or destroy this door (by being disobedient to ones father.)

The Rights of parent's after their demise:

Hadhrat Abu Saeed رضي الله تعالى عنه narrates that a person came to Nabi ﷺ and asked him, "My parents have passed away. Do they still have any rights upon me?" Nabi ﷺ said, "Yes, they do have rights upon you..........
1. Make dua that Allaah shows mercy to them.
2. Seek forgiveness on their behalf.
3. Fulfil the promises made by them.
4. Honour and respect their friends.
5. Do not cut of ties from their relatives." *(Ibn-Majah)*

Dear children. We now deem it necessary to mention those incidents by means of which you could learn how Nabi ﷺ treated his close relatives, foster mother, maternal aunt etc. We mention these so that we can ponder over them and practice upon them. In this way Allaah will surely be pleased with us.

Foster mother:

His ﷺ respect for Hadhrat Halima S'adiyah رضي الله تعالى عنها

Dear children. Let us look at the respect shown to his foster mother Halima S'adiyah رضي الله تعالى عنها.

On one occasion Rasulullaah ﷺ was seated with his companions when a woman arrived. He immediately stood up placing his shawl on the ground and saying, "Here my mother, here. **Please take a seat on this shawl!"** For as long as she remained seated he listened to her attentively and replied to her with utmost respect. When the time came for her to leave, he saw her off in a most respectful manner. The Sahaba رضي الله تعالى عنهم asked, "Who was that O Rasulullaah ﷺ?" He said, "That was my foster mother, Hadhrat Halima S'adiyah رضي الله تعالى عنها."

You see dear children? Our Nabi ﷺ practically demonstrated the manner in which we should show respect to our parents."

On another occasion Hadhrat Halima رضي الله تعالى عنها came to Nabi ﷺ complaining of droughts and famine in the area where she lived. **Nabi ﷺ presented her with forty goats and a camel laden with goods. (Tabaqat Ibn Sa'ad)**

Love shown to his foster father:

On one occasion, the husband of Hadhrat Halima رضي الله تعالى عنها, Harith رضي الله تعالى عنه, came to Makkah. The people went up to him and asked him, "Have you heard that your son claims that we will be resurrected after death?" Harith رضى الله تعالى عنه went to Nabi ﷺ and asked him if that which they were saying was true. **Nabi ﷺ most affectionately responded thus, "When that day comes, I will hold onto your hand and prove to you that whatever I had said was indeed true."** These words had such an effect on him that he immediately accepted Islaam. He later used to say, "Should my son grab hold of my hand, he will certainly not let go of it until I am entered into jannat." *(Seerat-un-Nabi ﷺ)*

Honouring his foster mother:

Nabi ﷺ used to show great respect to Hadhrat Umme Aiman رضى الله تعالى عنها who was the slave girl of his father. She had taken care of Nabi ﷺ during his childhood and used to see to the washing of his clothes and other needs. Nabi ﷺ used to respect her just as he would respect his mother. He would sometimes say, **"After my mother passed away, Umme Aiman رضى الله تعالى عنها is now like my mother."**

Kindness towards a maternal aunt:

A person came to Nabi ﷺ and requested that Nabi ﷺ makes dua for him. Nabi ﷺ advised him to show kindness towards his mother. The man said that his mother had passed away. **Nabi ﷺ then advised him to show kindness towards his maternal aunt.**

We learn that when parents pass away, one should show respect to the close relatives just as one would towards ones parents. **E.g. the maternal should be respected like a mother and the paternal uncle should be respected like a father.**

Respect shown to the mother of Hadhrat Ali ﷺ:

After the demise of the mother of Nabi ﷺ, the mother of Hadhrat Ali ﷺ, Hadhrat Fatima Bint Asadﷺ took Nabi ﷺ into her loving care. He also loved her very dearly.

When she passed away Nabi ﷺ gave his shawl (as a shroud) for her. He also lay in the grave so that through the blessings of Nubuwwat the grave would become a place of comfort and rest for her. After her burial he stood beside her grave for a while and made dua for her. Whilst making dua he said, "O my mother. May Allaah have mercy on you, for after the demise of my mother, you were like my mother. You would remain hungry so that I could eat. You would ensure that I had sufficient clothing when you were in greater need of clothing." Together with making dua for her, he would remember the goodness she had shown him. *(Al-Isabah)*

Chapter 6:

Sayings of Nabi ﷺ as regards the rights of children:

The rewards for correct upbringing of children:

A woman once came begging to Ummul Mu'mineen Hadhrat Aeysha رضى الله تعالى عنها. Accompanying her were her two daughters. At that moment in time Aeysha رضى الله تعالى عنها had nothing other than a single date to give the woman. She thus made over this single date.

The love of a mother in this poor woman for her children was such that she would not bare eating the date whilst her children went hungry. She therefore broke the date in two and made over a piece to each daughter. Seeing this, Aeysha رضى الله تعالى عنها was very much astonished. When Nabi ﷺ arrived she narrated to him what had occurred.

Hearing this Nabi ﷺ said, "Any person who is blessed with daughters and as a resulted tested (by Allaah), yet he/she shows kindness towards these daughters, **these daughters will serve as shields for that person against the fire of jahannam."** *(Muslim)*

The reward for bringing up two girls:

Nabi ﷺ is reported to have said that, "Any person who brings up two girls until they reach the age (where they are able to differentiate between right and wrong) will be this close to me on the Day of Judgement." (Nabi ﷺ indicated towards the closeness by holding up his two fingers close to one another.) *(Muslim)* Such a lofty position is indeed unimaginable.

On another occasion he said, "A father teaching his child a good manner is better than him giving one sa'a (approx. 4kgs) in charity."

On yet another occasion he said, "A father cannot give his child anything better than giving him sound (deeni) education." *(Thirmizi)*

In an effort to rectify the evil practice of giving preference to boys over girls, he once said, "That person who has been blessed with daughters and he does not kill them (by burying them alive as was an old Arab practice), neither does he humiliate them in any way, nor does he give preference to his sons over them (the daughters), will be given entry into jannat by Allaah." *(Sunan Abu-Dawud)*

Giving preference to sons over daughters or giving preference to one son over the other sons is also against the teachings of Islaam. This has been referred to as oppression by Rasulullaah ﷺ.

To make over all the wealth to one son thus depriving the other sons:

A Sahabi once gave only one of his sons a slave as a gift. He then came to Nabi ﷺ intending to make him a witness to this gift. Nabi ﷺ asked him if he had given all his sons a slave each. The man said that he had not done so. **Nabi ﷺ then said that he would never be witness to**

such an oppressive form of gifting. The man immediately desisted from his action. *(Sunan Abu-Dawud)*

It was a common practice amongst the Arabs to not only bury their daughters alive, but to kill their children due to financial difficulties. Islaam has strictly forbidden such behaviour and removed such practices from its very root. The Quraan instructs us thus, "And do not kill your children, fearing poverty." (Surah An'aam) When the responsibility of granting sustenance to parents and children is Allaahs' why should one then kill his children?

It was asked of Nabi ﷺ, "What is the greatest sin?" Nabi ﷺ said, "To ascribe any partners to Allaah." He was then asked, "Thereafter?" He said, "Disobedience towards parents." He was then asked, "Thereafter?" He said, "To kill ones children for fear of poverty." *(Sahih Muslim)*

This Hadith serves as advice towards both, parents and children. Children are advised to always be obedient to their parents, and parents are advised not to kill their children due to fear of poverty, rather they should consider children as a blessing from Allaah and thus give them a good upbringing.

Would my contribution towards charity on behalf of my Mother benefit her?

It has been reported on the authority of Bukhari Shareef that the mother of Hadhrat Sa'ad Ibn Ubaadah ﷺ had passed away and he was not present at the time. When he returned, he went to Nabi ﷺ and asked him, "Should I give charity on behalf of my late mother, would this then benefit her in any way?" Nabi ﷺ said, "Most certainly it will benefit her!" Hadhrat Sa'ad رضى الله تعالى عنه then told Nabi ﷺ that he was making him a witness to the fact that he had made over a certain orchard of his in charity, on behalf of his mother, which bore fruit in abundance. *(Bukhari)*

Dear children. **Would you not also like to give in charity on behalf of your parents after their demise, solely for the pleasure of Allaah?** Noble indeed are those children who emulate their predecessors by spending in good causes.

This Bedouin was my fathers' friend:

Hadhrat Abdullaah Ibn Umar رضى الله تعالى عنه was once travelling on the road to Makkah when he met a Bedouin along the way. He immediately mounted the Bedouin atop his mount and made over his turban to him. Those travelling with him were astonished at the amount of respect he had shown to this simple Bedouin. They told him that Bedouins are satisfied with much less. Why did he go out of his way to then honour an ordinary Bedouin? He told them that this Bedouin was his father, Umar Ibn Khattaabs' رضى الله تعالى عنه friend, which is why he had shown him such respect.

He then said, "I have heard Nabi ﷺ say that indeed it is from amongst the greatest of virtues to show kindness towards the friends of ones parents." *(Muslim)*

Only those children, who are obedient to their parents, will ever be kind and show respect towards their parents friends. As for those who are disobedient towards their parents, how will they ever practice on these Ahaadith?

Virtues of keeping children happy:

Remember, keeping your children happy is also an act of virtue which is reward able. We learn from the ahaadith that Nabi ﷺ has said, **"There is an abode in jannat known as the abode of happiness which is reserved for those who keep their children happy."** *(Kanzul-Ummaal)*

Keeping children happy implies that one should in keeping with the correct upbringing of children also laugh and joke with children. **In an appropriate manner one should also engage in permissible sport with children.** Incidents from the lives of the Ambiya ﷺ and pious should be narrated to them. Understanding them to be from amongst the many bounties of Allaah, one should approach them in a befitting manner. Allaah will certainly be pleased with one for doing this.

Children should not be allowed to go out when night falls:

Hadhrat Jaabir ﷺ narrates that Nabi ﷺ said, "When the night sets in do not allow your little children out doors as this is the time when the shayaateen spread out. Once some part of the night has passed you may let them out." *(Bukhari)*

Instructing children to perform their Salah:

Nabi ﷺ has instructed us that we should emphasize the importance of performing Salah to our children when they reach the age of seven and beat them (lightly without injuring them) if they neglect Salah at the age of ten. We should also separate their sleeping places when they have reached the age of ten. *(Abu-Dawud)*

That person who is unable to earn Jannat by service towards parents:

Hadhrat Abu Hurairah رضي الله تعالى عنه narrates that Nabi ﷺ said, "Cursed be that person! Disgraced be that person! Wretched be that person!" The Sahaba رضي الله تعالى عنهم asked, "Who?" Nabi ﷺ said, "That person who finds his parents or one of them in old age and yet fails to earn Jannat by serving them." *(Al-Adabul Mufrad)*

Dear children. Remember, serving ones parents will earn one Jannat and failure to do so will lead one to an evil fate and the fire of Jahannam. Therefore, whoever desires Jannat for himself should keep his/her parents happy by serving them. Allaah will certainly reward them with Jannat.

Allaah will increase his/her life span:

Hadhrat Sahal Ibn Muaaz narrates from his father Muaaz رضي الله تعالى عنه that Nabi ﷺ said, "Allaah will increase the life span of that person who treats his parents with kindness." *(Al-Adabul Mufrad)*

What one should do in the event of ones parent/s being non Muslims:

When Hadhrat Sa'ad Ibn Abi Waqaas رضي الله تعالى عنه accepted Islaam, his mother took an oath that she will not eat or drink until he denounces Islaam. Hadhrat Sa'ad told her that there was no way he was going to denounce Islaam. His mother was firm on her oath and therefore did not eat or drink anything for three days! Hadhrat Sa'ad then told her that even if she were to be given a hundred lives and she destroyed each one of them in this way, he was not going to denounce Islaam therefore she should give up and begin eating. She finally gave up and began eating. *(Adabul-Mufrad)*

The verse of the Quraan was then revealed that one should not obey his/her parents if they instruct him/her to ascribe partners with Allaah, but one should still deal with them kindly in worldly matters.

We learn that a person should always be obedient to his/her parents if they are believers. One should also be kind, show respect, obey and listen to ones parents if they are non Muslims, but one cannot obey them if they instruct one to ascribe partners with Allaah or order them to do anything contrary to the teachings of Allaah and his Rasulﷺ.

Translation Edited by
Mufti Afzal Hoosen Elias
Muharaam 1431-January-2010

NOTE